Pierrre F. Lebeurier

Life of Rev. Mother Saint Joseph, foundress of the Congregation of Sisters of St. Joseph of Bordeaux

By L'abbe P. F. Lebeurier; translated from the French by a Sister of St. Joseph

Pierrre F. Lebeurier

Life of Rev. Mother Saint Joseph, foundress of the Congregation of Sisters of St. Joseph of Bordeaux
By L'abbe P. F. Lebeurier; translated from the French by a Sister of St. Joseph

ISBN/EAN: 9783337733407

Printed in Europe, USA, Canada, Australia, Japan

Cover: Foto ©ninafisch / pixelio.de

More available books at **www.hansebooks.com**

LIFE

OF

REV. MOTHER SAINT JOSEPH,

FOUNDRESS OF THE

Congregation of Sisters of St. Joseph

OF BORDEAUX.

BY

L'ABBÉ P. F. LEBEURIER,

Canon of Evreux and Keeper of the Seals of Eure.

TRANSLATED FROM THE FRENCH

BY

A SISTER OF ST. JOSEPH.

NEW YORK:
D. & J. SADLIER & CO., 31 BARCLAY ST.
MONTREAL: 275 NOTRE DAME STREET.

1876.

APPROBATION

OF

HIS EMINENCE CARDINAL DONNET,

Archbishop of Bordeaux.

We, Ferdinand Francis Augustin Donnet, by the grace of God and the Apostolic See Cardinal Priest of the Holy Roman Catholic Church, Archbishop of Bordeaux, Primate of Aquitaine.

We hereby approve the book entitled " Life of Mother St. Joseph, Foundress of the Sisters of St. Joseph at Bordeaux."

This work, which recommends itself by the beauty of its diction, appears to us worthy of perusal, on account of the recital of the virtues of this Superior, as well as the summary of an administration signalized by wisdom and visibly assisted by Heaven.

Mother St. Joseph was a model of a perfect religious to her community, and to the world she gave examples of piety and charity. We are pleased to recommend this life as a collection of

Approbation.

beautiful lessons offered to all souls desirous of advancing in perfection, to all the houses of religious in the diocese, and particularly to the Sisters of St. Joseph at Bordeaux.

Given at Bordeaux, July 2, 1869.

✠ F. C. D., Archbishop.

APPROBATION OF BISHOP DEVONCOUX.

EVREUX, August 5, 1869.

My Dear Curé:

I have read with as much interest as attention the "Life of Mother St. Joseph." I authorize its publication, and recommend it to be read. Religious souls will find therein great encouragement in the practice of the virtues of their holy state, and the faithful will recognize the wisdom and power of God in the means made use of in advancing his glory, in the education of youth, and the salvation of souls.

Receive, dear Curé, a new assurance of my devotion.

✠ JOHN, Bishop of Evreux.

ABBE LEBEURIER, HON. CANON OF EVREUX, RECTOR OF GRAVIGNY.

AUTHOR'S PREFACE.

MY acquaintance with the worthy religious whose life I write commenced in 1845. A humble and holy priest, Father Bonet, whose memory still lives in the hearts of those who knew him, had frequently spoken to me of Mother St. Joseph, for whom he entertained a sincere regard. I embraced an opportunity of making her acquaintance with pleasure, being, however, on my guard against admitting the impression which Father Bonet's account of her works had made on me. As soon as the good Mother spoke to me all reserve vanished. Her words and manner evinced so much simplicity, united with dignity and affability, that one felt immediately attracted to her with unlimited confidence. Having arranged the affair which took me thither, the con-

versation turned on various topics, and finally on prayer. She spoke of confidence in God in prayer with so much unction that I was deeply touched by her words. In listening to her it seemed to me that I understood fully for the first time the most familiar texts of the Gospel. That simple conversation made so strong an impression on me that for a long time after I occupied myself, though reluctantly, with the subject of which she spoke. I saw the venerable Superior several times afterwards, and she became to me a mother whose pious and affectionate counsels and untiring zeal are among the sweetest remembrances of my life.

A personal incident, which I may relate here, will give an idea of the frankness of her character, the kindness of her heart, and the nature of the relations we held. In 1849 she requested me to give the general retreat to her community. For some years previous I had been employed as Professor of Moral and Dogmatic Theology at Bordeaux, and I had acquired in that function a facility for speaking in public; but I was still quite young and wanting in experience of the inner working of souls, and, above all, of the knowledge necessary to the director of a retreat.

I at once refused her request; but the good Mother insisted so urgently on my compliance that I was forced to yield to her wish. I made all possible preparation, not, however, without much uneasiness as to the consequences. At the opening of the retreat, after my first sermon, which was listened to with great attention, I returned to my room well satisfied with my success. In a few moments the Mother followed me, and, without any ceremony, said: "Father, if you continue the retreat in this style, all the fruit is lost. Put aside your flowery sermons; we are not *literati*, but simple religious, assembled to occupy our minds with the affairs of our salvation. It is necessary only to set before us pious truths which will raise our hearts to God, remind us of our duties, know our defects, and correct them."

It is easier to imagine than describe the effect produced by this equivocal compliment; but the good Mother immediately apologized, and remedied my want of experience in retreat-giving by her practical counsels.

At the time of her death I had left Bordeaux, but have several times since given the annual retreat to her community. In 1857, at the urgent request of her sisters in religion and of her nephew, Father Montcenis, I commenced to write her life. All her private papers and a voluminous correspondence were delivered to me, and I made an analytical abstract and placed them in chronological order. I have questioned all the religious who were acquainted with their foundress, and obtained the written testimony of her assistant concerning all her actions since 1838, besides having the recollections of her most intimate confidant, Sister Immaculate Conception. Others, too, who had been recipients of favors through her prayers or works, remitted letters in testimony of these. It is from these sources I obtained the facts related in the publication. The authority on which a statement is made is generally given, and where no testimony is stated the fact is personally known either to myself or Sister Immaculate Conception.

After the glory of God, ever admirable in His saints, my principal object in publishing this life is to cancel a debt of gratitude I owe to Mother St. Joseph, and to give a mark of my interest and regard for her community. It is at their request, and for them especially, that I write; hence many details will be found which are of no importance to strangers, but of great interest to Mother St. Joseph's daughters.

I also wish to contribute to the edification of Christian souls and to the instruction of persons bound by the vows of religion. I trust in the divine goodness that they will read many beautiful examples of piety and charity, and spiritual maxims marked with the seal of wisdom and common sense. The religious of the Congregation of St. Joseph, of every community, will find therein the true spirit of their pious founder, and the details of the origin and growth of their institute. Many facts in the following account seem rather extraordinary for a man devoted to works of erudition, and accustomed to the severest proceedings of historical criticism, to admit without difficulty. In answer to this objection I will say: The supernatural is the very essence of Christianity. Our actual life, according to the teachings of the Church, is but a preparation for another and a better life, in which the faculties of our souls and the organization of our bodies will be changed, not by the play of natural forces, which constitutes terrestrial transformations, but by a new impulse directly from God and added to the primitive forces of our nature. This transformation of our present life will have its perfection only in heaven, but its germ, its supernatural principle, is deposited in our souls in this world. This supernatural principle is the grace of God, the divine element that mingles with our free-will, diffuses in our mind lights superior to those of reason, opens our intellect to the understanding of divine mysteries, detaches us from terrestrial things, directs our will towards eternity, and excites in our hearts aspirations for heavenly joys.

The impulse of grace leads us not only to seek for the mysterious principle of nature, not alone to see God as our natural capacity allows—that is, through the veil of creation, by forming in ourselves a higher idea of Him from the knowledge obtained in the sciences that investigate the material world—but it seeks to go still further, and penetrate through and beyond creation, and there contemplate God, our Principle and our End, such as He is in His divine essence, and live united with Him for ever in the splendor of intellectual light, in transports of love, joy, and gratitude. This union will doubtless be realized in heaven, where our faculties will be capable of fully enjoying it; but it begins here below amid shadows which are best adapted to time of trial. God lives supernaturally in our souls by His grace; and He unites Himself with us in the holy sacrament of His love. The most lowly Christian is favored with intimate and supernatural communications from God; and daily facts prove the working of prodigies by the Creator for the good of the creature. The graces of the sacraments are standing miracles. It is, then, a strange illusion and an unjustifiable mode of reasoning that directs the sceptic of the age to reject the belief in miracles, apparitions, ecstasies, and extraordinary communications from God.

From a critical point of view, marvellous incidents give rise to two questions: 1st. Are the facts consistent in themselves? 2d. Do they present a character that may be attributed to natural causes? The first question presents no difficulty whatever. All historical facts rest on testimony, and the critic receives or rejects them according to the veracity of the narrator. I designate the source whence I derive the facts, and leave the reader at full liberty to admit or discard them. The lives of the saints, written by great and learned men, such as St. Jerome, Theodoret, Athanasius, and many modern writers, abound in facts which, taken on the whole, are certainly beyond natural causes; but are the incidents miraculous? It is often difficult to determine, and the proof is seldom necessary. The son of a fond mother is apparently dying; human skill can do nothing for him; his mother makes a vow, offers fervent prayers to God, and he immediately recovers. Is this a miracle? The happy mother is tempted to believe it is. Possibly a natural and unexpected crisis brought about his recovery. The mother does not enquire into this, but gives thanks to God, who is the author of the natural as well as supernatural order.

On the contrary, when a recovery is given as a miracle, in proof of the sanctity of a person by whom it was obtained, the critic not only has a right, but it is his duty, to examine carefully every fact connected with it. He will admit the supernatural character only when the recovery is proved to be incontestable and inconsistent with natural laws; otherwise the decision is against the miraculous character, and it is rejected as proof. The Church acts in this manner in the process of canonization. But in writing the life of Mother St. Joseph my intention is not to prove miracles. There will occur frequent accounts of visions and apparitions and other incidents, received on the testimony of the pious Mother herself. It is to be presumed that she gave these only after having seriously examined from what source they proceeded, and, being guided by Christian wisdom, she would make account of lights and graces received only with prudence and reserve.

For my part, I have been guided solely on the principle of truth. If, under pretext of historical criticism, I should have omitted all that bears a marvellous appearance, I should have changed the nature of the life I undertook to portray, and have described Mother St. Joseph in a way that even her spiritual daughters would not have known her. I have, then, closely presented an exact picture of her character, her spirit, the habits of her life, and the influence she exercised on those around her. After what I have just said, it is scarcely necessary for me to add, in order to conform myself to the rules of the Church, that in giving the title of saint, venerable, and analogous terms either to Mother St. Joseph or other persons, I mean to designate persons of piety, and not to prevent the judgments of the Holy See, to which I shall ever submit my sentiments, my writings, and my life.

CONTENTS.

CHAPTER I.
Birth and Parentage, ... 21

CHAPTER II.
Her first Confession, ... 26

CHAPTER III.
Her early Education, ... 32

CHAPTER IV.
Her Mother cultivates in the Soul of Jane great Devotion to the most Blessed Sacrament, . 38

CHAPTER V.
The Blessed Virgin teaches her the use of Instruments of Penance, ... 41

CHAPTER VI.
Her Entrance into a Religious Community, . . 45

CHAPTER VII.
Her Temptations, ... 49

CHAPTER VIII.
Death of Madame Chanay, ... 53

CHAPTER IX.

Mademoiselle Chanay resides with her Sister after the Death of her Mother—Her Works of Charity, ... 56

CHAPTER X.

Her Vocation to the Religious Life, . . . 60

CHAPTER XI.

Origin of the Sisters of St. Joseph—Established at Puy 1650—Growth of Institute—Dispersion of Sisters, 1790—Their re-establishment in the Diocese of Lyons, 1807, ... 64

CHAPTER XII.

Her Novitiate, ... 73

CHAPTER XIII.

Sister St. Joseph at Chazay, ... 78

CHAPTER XIV.

Her Works at Belley, ... 87

CHAPTER XV.

Her Spirit of Poverty and great Confidence in Divine Providence, ... 92

CHAPTER XVI.

Monseigneur Devie nominated Bishop of Belley—Mother St. Joseph appointed Superior-General of the Sisters of St. Joseph, . . . 98

CHAPTER XVII.

Difficulties experienced by Mother St. Joseph in her Administration—Founding of divers Industrial Schools at Belley, ... 103

CHAPTER XVIII.
Foundation of the House at Ferney, . . . 108

CHAPTER XIX.
Her Recovery on St. Anthelme's Day—Favors obtained by her Prayers, ... 112

CHAPTER XX.
Foundation of a House of Providence for the Aged and Orphans—Her Charity towards Them, . 122

CHAPTER XXI.
She fulfils the Duties of Assistant, . . . 132

CHAPTER XXII.
Her Zeal in favoring Vocations to the Priesthood, 142

CHAPTER XXIII.
Progress of Mother St. Joseph in the Spiritual Life, 152

CHAPTER XXIV.
Mother St. Joseph founds the Congregation at Gap, ... 164

CHAPTER XXV.
Her arrival at Gap—Visit of Bishop Devie, . . 173

CHAPTER XXVI.
Conversion of two Young Girls at Marseilles, . 183

CHAPTER XXVII.
Foundation of Remollen, ... 193

CHAPTER XXVIII.
New Foundations, ... 201

CHAPTER XXIX.
Mother St. Joseph goes to Bordeaux, . . . 208

CHAPTER XXX.
Mother St. Joseph establishes her Order at Barsac, 219

CHAPTER XXXI.
Arrival of Sister St. Paul, ... 228

CHAPTER XXXII.
Her Care of the Sick, ... 237

CHAPTER XXXIII.
She renews a Request to establish a Novitiate at Bordeaux, ... 247

CHAPTER XXXIV.
Generosity of the Archbishop, ... 255

CHAPTER XXXV.
Purchase of a Convent at Bordeaux, . . . 268

CHAPTER XXXVI.
Novitiate at Bordeaux, ... 279

CHAPTER XXXVII.
Her Principles on the Reception of Novices— Father Taillefer nominated Superior, . . 293

CHAPTER XXXVIII.
Her Zeal for the Observance of Rule, . . . 304

CHAPTER XXXIX.
Letters of Bishop Devie—Mother St. Joseph visits Bourg, Belley, and Ars, ... 312

CHAPTER XL.
New Edition of Rules, ... 325

CHAPTER XLI.
Last general Retreat presided over by Mother St. Joseph—Her last Illness and Death, . . 340

APPENDIX, ... 359

LIFE OF
REV. MOTHER SAINT JOSEPH.

CHAPTER I.

BIRTH AND PARENTAGE.

DIVERSITY characterizes all the works of God's creation, and is particularly manifest in His saints, whose virtues ever shine resplendent in Christianity's horizon, guiding-stars to the wayfarer journeying through the night of life. The light of many is for a time obscured by the heavy clouds of sin and passion, but the obscurity is followed by the mild refulgence of humble penitence, reflecting a mercy all divine, while at the same time it sheds rays of hope and courage in the path of the despondent. Other saints by predilection are ever radiant in the sunshine of God's love, from the cradle recipients of Heaven's choicest gifts, and, shadowed through life by preventive grace, are restored to their Creator with not a maze to dim their lustrous brightness; and in this latter class is ranked Jane Chanay, known as Reverend Mother St. Joseph.

She was born at Villefranche, of pious and respectable parents, and was the twenty-fourth child in a family of twenty-one sons and three daughters. Her father, Mark Chanay, was a hatter by trade, and was remarkable both for his superior intellectual endowments and an integrity which won the respect and esteem of all who knew him. Her mother, in whose character was blended great goodness of heart, amiable sweetness of manner, tender compassion for the poor, and an animated faith that firmly sustained her in the midst of the most trying difficulties, was a model to all Christian women. The breaking out of the French Revolution spread devastation throughout the kingdom, and carried terror into the homes of the royalists. M. Chanay, being enthusiastically devoted to the cause of his sovereign, incurred the hatred of the revolutionists, and was, with many others, obliged to seek refuge and safety in Spain. His wife remained at Villefranche, charged with the care and support of her numerous family. With war and its attendant famine raging both at home and abroad, one would suppose the task of maintaining and educating her children would be too great for the strength and capacity of a woman. Notwithstanding these and many other evils, Madame Chanay labored with almost superhuman courage, founded on great confidence in God, and surmounted every obstacle. Day and night her every energy was strained to supply the wants of her children, and, instigated by her maternal love and devotedness, she frequently denied herself necessaries of life to lessen their privations.

The unbounded fury of the revolutionists was wreaked on everything stamped with the religion of Jesus Christ. Churches were closed or razed to the ground, priests dispersed or guillotined, altars desecrated, and every religious rite prohibited. Reason was the watchword, and the tenets of Voltaire superseded the maxims of the Gospel.

Deeply afflicted at the triumph of impiety, and powerless to aid in the restoration of God's altars, she made in her own dwelling an oratory, where every moment of the day prayers were offered to His offended majesty. At times, when she learned that Mass was to be celebrated by one of the persecuted ministers of the Church in some obscure hiding-place, she went to assist at the Holy Sacrifice without even a thought of the danger, and even death, consequent on discovery. She would have forfeited life a thousand times for the privilege of receiving Jesus Christ in the most holy sacrament of the altar. Fears for the safety and welfare of her husband constantly disturbed her peace, and, with the intention of obtaining his return to his family, she besought the divine Solace of all woes to accept the offering of the child she bore, and promised to consecrate it to His service. Shortly after this God revealed to her that her desire would be fulfilled, and that she should give birth to a daughter who would be the spiritual mother of numerous virgins consecrated to Him.

This child was Jane. She was born on the 12th of January, 1795. Despite the dark clouds of oppression that overshadowed her country during the Reign of

Terror, and the sad forebodings for the future that filled her heart, the birth of her child was a source of joy to the pious mother. She loved her with a love of preference, and from the first dawn of intelligence she endeavored to develop in her soul the germs of faith and piety. Unhappily for the child, her mother made no effort to conceal the special love she entertained for her, and a knowledge of its existence excited dissatisfaction among the older children. They called Jane the Joseph of the family; taunts and reproaches were heaped upon her; and at last harsh treatment was carried so far that it was found necessary to send her away from home.

CHAPTER II.

HER FIRST CONFESSION.

WHEN once the fire of jealousy is kindled in a soul, nothing can satiate its ravages until the object of the passion be removed. Reason is blinded, the heart hardened, and the whole character embittered by the presence of the supposed preferred one. Having a perfect knowledge of the dispositions of her older children towards Jane, and, moreover, being convinced that but one course was open to her, she sacrificed her personal inclinations, and resolved to place her child under the care of Madame Mignone, Jane's godmother. This lady's château was situated at Lima, a short distance from Villefranche. Her godchild was welcomed to her new home with the greatest kindness, and every attention lavished on her. Her precocious intellect, lively imagination, and joyous manner, her ready answers and loving heart, made her an object of interest and affection to the whole household. Her every wish was gratified.

The pious teachings of her mother had made an ineffaceable impression on the mind of the child, and in the midst of the innocent pleasures that surrounded her she complained she had not time to pray. Often when visitors came to the château she hid herself, and, on being called to account for her absence, she always answered that she loved to converse alone with God.

An idea to make a hermitage for herself entered her mind, and, with the impulsive ardor that even at that early age had shown itself to be one of her characteristic traits, the design was immediately carried out. On the grounds adjoining the house she had noticed a large gooseberry bush covered with inviting red berries. This she considered a retreat to her purpose, and the fruit would serve her as food. She counted the berries, resolved to eat every day a limited number, and her calculations promised sufficient nourishment for several weeks. But, alas! for childish resolves when hunger claimed its right. Quite early in the morning she ate the determined number; at noon she took a few more, excusing herself for exceeding the limit on the plea that they looked larger than they tasted. The afternoon hours wore on slowly and heavily, and when evening came the bush was completely stripped of its berries. Still the would-be hermit longed for more, and was forced to abandon her solitude to satisfy the craving for a substantial meal. She was, however, by no means discouraged at her want of firmness, but promised herself greater constancy in the future. This childish project foreshadowed her inclinations to a religious life and to obedience, and showed, moreover, her appreciation of solitude and intimate converse with God.

When about eight years of age, while visiting a church one day in company with her nurse, her attention was attracted by seeing persons going in and out of the confessional. She asked the girl what they were doing in that little house, and, on being told that a minister of God and representative of Jesus Christ heard the confessions of persons and gave them pardon of their sins, she immediately declared she wanted to go to confession.

The girl told her that she was not prepared to approach the sacrament, and her godmother would be displeased if she did so; but her remonstrances were in vain. Jane would not be deterred from carrying out her will. She pulled the dress of the lady in the confessional, and said aloud: "Madam, you are there long enough; please come out and allow me in to confess my sins." Not being obeyed at once, she continued her request, and pulled the harder at the dress, until the place was left free. On entering the confessional she told her sins with so much candor and precision that the confessor asked her questions that spiritual persons advanced in years, but less enlightened in the ways of God, would have found difficulty in answering; but the child replied clearly and without a shade of embarrassment.

The priest who heard this her first confession was Father Fauvette, subsequently well known as a great missionary in France. He directed her until her entrance into religion, and always entertained great interest in her, confident that she was destined by God to tread the higher paths of spiritual life. After confessing her sins she consulted him concerning her manner of life with her godmother, which she regarded as worldly and imperfect, and was far from being contented with it. "Father," she asked, "will this life of ease and pleasure lead me to heaven?" He answered: "My child, we can save our souls in any condition of life. Be good and obedient, pray often, and have great confidence in God." This advice was not satisfactory to the little girl, and she said: "Father, reflect on what you have told me. On Judgment-day you will be accountable for my soul to its Creator. Tell me, then, does God wish me to continue this life of self-indulgence, and will it take me to Him, whom I wish to serve at any cost?" The confessor, still more astonished, replied: "Return to your mother, and be directed by the inspirations of grace which God will never fail to send you." This instance showed that obedience was to be her favorite virtue. She felt it would be useless to ask permission to leave her godmother, who had learned to love her as her own child, and she resolved to go from the house without acquainting any one with her intention. Being naturally of a grateful and affectionate disposition, this act called for a great sacrifice on her part; for she knew her conduct would appear ungrateful and cause sorrow to those who long had cherished her. Nature was forced to yield to the call of duty, and she secretly left the home that had sheltered her for years, to return to her parents, with whom she remained until their death.

CHAPTER III.

HER EARLY EDUCATION.

JANE'S return to the parental roof was as agreeable to the wishes of her devoted parents and pleasing to them as it was to herself. Her mother's heart had always yearned towards her with a longing that only a mother can know, and a reciprocal attraction drew the daughter towards the heart that most loved her. The feelings of jealousy that caused her banishment had been softened by time, and her brothers and sisters tolerated her as a sharer of their privileges without an emotion of envy. The quick perception of the mother at once saw this change in their conduct, and she applied herself with renewed energy to form the character of her daughter to piety, and directed her every inclination and affection to God as the source of all good and the only object deserving her fullest love. She carefully explained the principal mysteries of religion, and gave her daily task-lessons from the Scriptures. Moreover, she obliged her to read the lives of the saints, and afterwards to tell her what was most pleasing and striking in them, and of what virtues they gave particular example. This early education laid the foundation of that perfect knowledge of the Holy Scriptures for which later in life she, as Mother St. Joseph, was remarkable. She could then, with the greatest facility, always use an appropriate text of Scripture to exemplify any assertion made, and their use naturally flowed into her ordinary conversation. When persons expressed surprise at this, she told them her mother's teachings had graved them in her memory, and they remained indelibly fixed therein. In her spiritual conferences with her religious she frequently explained mysteries of religion or spoke of the virtues that shone in the life of the saint commemorated, and added: "My mother taught me this lesson years ago to-day, while instructing me in my catechism." At this tender age her mo ther initiated her into the practice of interior recollection and mental prayer. She taught her to erect an oratory in her soul, where our divine Lord could incessantly receive the tribute of her adoration and love. This intimate union of her soul with Jesus became so natural to the child that nothing could distract her mind from a sense of the presence of God, and this union was maintained without detriment to the exterior joy, happiness, and agreeable liberty of spirit and engaging manner that throughout her life attracted all that came under her influence. Though ignorant of her mother's vow to consecrate her to God, she early evinced a decided inclination to become a religious. Her favorite amusement was to dress dolls as Sisters, and play the mother-superior over them. But the dolls soon proved insufficient subjects for the zealous, aspiring teacher, as even then she experienced an uncontrollable desire to labor for the salvation of souls. Accordingly, she assembled a number of children about her own age, taught them the catechism, spoke to them of death, judgment, hell, and heaven, picturing them in colors so glowing, vivid, and forcible as to elicit from her child audience a unanimous "We will not deserve hell"; and when she fully excited their interest, her eloquent tongue would exhort them to shun evil company, avoid sin, be good and obedient, and thereby merit heaven, thus early manifesting her fitness for the career of zeal and charity to which afterwards full scope was given.

Her love for the poor was almost a passion, and her charity towards them was often carried to excess. She always gave them the spending-money that was given her; and whenever she could dispose of her own meals unperceived, she laid them aside for the earliest applicant.

Still, she was by no means faultless. The principal element in her nature was a pride which fostered a will to control everything and make all subservient to her. Whenever she was thwarted in this point, or even the least resistance opposed to her will, she immediately gave way to a violent anger that brought on fits of insensibility. Her mother was for a time greatly alarmed, in the dread that her daughter was afflicted with an incurable malady; but on consulting a physician he assured her that the fit was occasioned by ungovernable temper alone, and she took courage to apply an effective remedy, making use of every opportunity to show the child the heinous guilt of this sin. Anger, she said, is a monster that makes those who yield to it resemble beasts in depriving them of the use of reason. A little girl in anger is an object of horror in the sight of God, who is infinite goodness and ineffable sweetness. On the contrary, He contemplates with delight a child that does violence to herself and overcomes this passion; and Mary, our loving Mother, with the angels and saints, are pleased at beholding the efforts she makes and the sacrifices she endures to please Jesus Christ. These reasonings made a deep impression on the heart of the child, and elicited resolutions of amendment; but for a long time every contradiction was followed by a repetition of a fault. In these instances her mother would await the return of calm, then renew her lesson of meekness, and encourage the child by telling her that she perceived great improvement in her temper, and that God would assist her to entirely overcome herself if she asked His grace and continued her efforts. She, moreover, told her to make her examen of conscience every day on the virtue of patience, to impose a penance on herself for every fault against it, and to give her an account of her falls and of her victories over self. By these means she overcame the passion of anger before it became too deeply rooted in her soul.

CHAPTER IV.

HER MOTHER CULTIVATES IN THE SOUL OF JANE GREAT DEVOTION TO THE MOST BLESSED SACRAMENT.

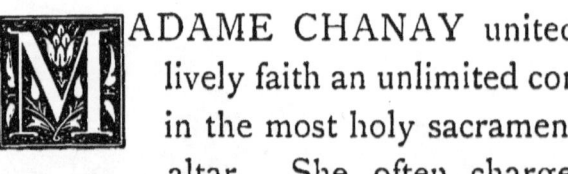ADAME CHANAY united with a lively faith an unlimited confidence in the most holy sacrament of the altar. She often charged Jane to go with messages to the sacred Presence in the tabernacle, and return to her with whatever answer should be given her soul. The child obeyed her mother's wishes simply, and frequently remained for hours before the altar, where her faith and perseverance were often rewarded with extraordinary favors.

Being ten years of age, and as the time for making her first communion approached, the pious mother left nothing undone on her part to fully instruct her child for the reception of this most holy sacrament. She taught her to adorn her soul with the practice of virtues, which she should incessantly cultivate, that her heart might resemble a delightful garden wherein choicest plants would exhale the agreeable odor of fragrant perfume. She told her that her soul was soon to become a tabernacle, in which, as in a living ciborium, the God-Man, lover of human hearts, would delight to dwell. She said: " Purify this ciborium by a sincere and contrite confession of all your sins. If you detest them, your soul will be a dwelling clean and pure, wherein the Lamb without spot will delight to remain. He dwelleth among the lilies. Be stainless as this lovely flower of the field, and you will attract His love." Inexpressible joy filled her soul on the morning of the day of her first communion, and an intense longing for the moment when God would unite Himself to her so absorbed all her faculties that nothing could divert her thoughts from the great act about to be accomplished. Her mother was, on her part, desirous of making her child an example of modesty and simplicity in dress, and for the purpose studiously avoided all display. The child wore a plain white dress and a veil, with a crown of white roses as the only ornament.

When she received the sacred species, her heart was overwhelmed with an undefined sweetness and filled with a hitherto unexperienced calm and joy. She afterwards said that on that day she begged the reception of three graces: the first, to communicate every day; the second, to become a religious; and the third, to become a saint. "The first two," she said, "were granted me, and the other I am endeavoring to obtain." From this time forward she was more closely united to God, more desirous of doing good, and manifested a longing for the practice of almost incredible interior mortification and corporal austerities.

CHAPTER V.

THE BLESSED VIRGIN TEACHES HER THE USE OF INSTRUMENTS OF PENANCE.

S the Advent succeeding her first communion neared, Jane felt herself drawn to the love of virtue and the practice of corporal austerities. She purposed to prepare herself for the coming feast of Christmas by some extraordinary acts of virtue, that she might be rewarded in the coming of the infant Jesus into her soul; and, as she considered mortification of self most pleasing to God, she asked instruction in the matter from her mother. Madame Chanay was pleased with the manifest predispositions to virtue in her child, and she allowed her to practise some mild penances which prudence suggested would not be injurious to the health of her daughter. Jane, knowing that her mother's affection would not allow her to act freely in

the matter, and not content with the ordinary austerities named to her, resolved to have recourse to the Blessed Virgin to teach her the penances performed by the saints. She who ever lends a willing ear to the petitions of innocence and confidence inspired the child to go to a Lyonese family and to procure a discipline, a hair shirt and a cilice. Jane managed to go alone to Lyons, and on her way there kept repeating the names of the instruments of penance. On reaching the house designated she asked the woman in attendance if she sold those articles, and was answered in the negative. Jane repeated her question, and added that she would pay any amount for them. The woman then showed Jane into an inner apartment, and, taking from a drawer instruments of various kinds, asked which she wished to purchase. The child said, "Give me one of each," and took them from the woman, to whom she gave eight francs for the new toys, and hastened home, delighted with her success.

Advent having commenced, she formed the resolve to use these instruments of penance regularly, and to limit her food to three boiled potatoes, or their equivalent, every day, except Sunday, until Christmas. She studiously concealed all her austerities from her mother. Together with these practices she applied herself to interior mortification and prayer. Her mother had taught her to place herself under the guidance of St. Joseph, to invoke his aid, and to study him as the grand and perfect model of the interior life. During all this season she united herself in spirit with the Blessed Virgin and St. Joseph, adoring the Incarnate God; and frequently, in the excess of simplicity and confidence, she would say, " Mary, my Mother, let my heart be His cradle ; cloth emy soul with your virtues, and He will delight to dwell in it and remain sole possessor for ever."

Christmas eve seemed an age to her. At midnight Mass her heart burned with expectation and seemed as if breaking. When the bell announced the solemn moment of the consecration, her eyes were rivetted on the altar, and she beheld there the figure of a most beautiful Child, surrounded by a dazzling brightness. She could plainly discern His countenance, resplendent with light;

His hands shed luminous rays, and were extended as if blessing. At this sight she fainted and was carried home insensible. The physician who was called in could attribute her condition only to a supernatural cause. She remained in ecstasy for twelve hours. This vision preluded many others, and she always preserved a tender devotion to the infant Jesus. Through the whole course of her life she spoke of Jesus in most affectionate terms peculiarly her own.

CHAPTER VI.

HER ENTRANCE INTO A RELIGIOUS COMMUNITY.

WHEN only twelve years of age, Jane felt a desire to consecrate herself to God in the religious state. As in every other instance of her life, she was also in this anxious to put her intention into immediate execution. Her pleadings were so urgent that her mother sought admittance for her into a religious community. She, however, asked the Sisters to employ her daughter in menial and difficult labors, calculated to convince her by experience that as yet the duties of community life were above her strength. The Sisters faithfully complied with the mother's request. They required Jane to work constantly, and assigned her all the drudgery of the house. Not having been accustomed to labor at home, these new duties were attended with results most painful to nature. Still, her energy was not in the least diminished nor her ardor cooled. However, her quick perception soon observed a marked difference between the food, clothing, and general condition of the choir and the lay Sisters, and this fact determined her not to make this order her religious haven. She was surprised to find what she considered a spirit of disunion, pride, and selfishness prevail where she expected to find only charity, humility, and self-sacrifice. When, after a few weeks' stay at the convent, her sister-in-law came to visit her, she willingly returned to her mother. She afterwards said: "I left without a shade of regret a house whence was banished the spirit of humility, confident that God would one day call me to an order whose members would mutually render assistance and be the servants of one another." God, whose designs are inscrutable, preserved these dispositions in her soul, and the trials to which she was subjected became for her treasures of experience from which she derived great profit.

From this time until her mother's death she remained at home. She learned from her mother the practice of all virtues, but particularly the exercise of charity towards the needy and distressed. These ever found in both mother and daughter a ready sympathy and willingness to encourage and relieve. Jane generally followed her impulses, and was frequently led by them to go beyond ordinary bounds in her desire to assist all who came in her way. During a short visit to her brother at Lyons, she one day heard the hoarse voice of an old man singing beneath the window. On looking out she saw the singer, a poor, blind man, scarce covered with rags, and led by a dog. She immediately went to the man, and, taking his hand, led him through the city, and sang with him at every place they expected a pittance for their endeavors. She spent several hours in this exercise of mercy, and returned to her family with a contented heart, after having obtained a considerable sum for the beggar. Often, in after-life, when a similar necessity called for the exercise of charity, she felt moved by the same impulse, but years brought a prudence that deterred her. She related this as one of her extravagances, but the Sisters recorded it in memory with all the other incidents gleaned from her conversations and relating to her youth; they hoping that God would one day proclaim to the world the sanctity of His servant.

Love of God so filled her heart that she desired with an intense longing to die, that she might behold Him as He is known to the blessed. Regarding death as the gate to eternity, she longed for it, and at each Holy Communion she besought God to open the door that separated her from His presence. Having a presentiment that her prayers were about to be heard, she went to her confessor and joyfully said to him: "Father, I am going to die this year; our Lord has told me."

"Has he told you what kind of death?" asked the director.

"No; but I am going to die soon."

"Very well; there are two deaths for you, and it is death to self-love you are now to realize."

She went away saddened at the disappointment, but fully resolved to accomplish this death and leave no obstacle to the perfect fulfilment of the will of her divine Master.

CHAPTER VII.

HER TEMPTATIONS.

THE way to heaven is marked by lights and shadows in alternate succession, and the heavenly lights and graces bestowed on Jane were followed by periods of darkness and temptation. She gives the following account of one of the many trials to which her soul was subjected: "When about seventeen years of age, I was one day assailed by evil thoughts. In an instant my mind was flooded with imaginations the like of which I had never before experienced. I shrank with horror from myself, and felt utterly unworthy to associate with creatures. All within me seemed confusion and darkness, and I believed myself lost. My will alone remained firm in the resolve rather to die than commit even a venial sin; but I was scarcely conscious of this feeling. I had recourse to Jesus in the Blessed Sacrament; but He seemed deaf to my petitions, and I said to myself, I am become an object of horror and disgust to Him. I could only weep and pray. At last I besought the intercession of my Mother Mary, and earnestly prayed her to come to my assistance. During all the time I did my utmost to divert my thoughts, and with this purpose I worked until, weak and almost fainting, I sank into a chair, and, resting my head on a table, fell into a slumber, during which I dreamed that the Blessed Virgin appeared to me, carrying in her arms the child Jesus. He smiled graciously, and directed His Mother's attention to me. Both Mother and Child invited me to approach, and my heart burned with desire to join them. The way leading to them was covered by thorns and briers, that wounded my hands and feet at every step; but nothing could retard me on my way nor lessen my desire to arrive at my destination. Occasionally I raised my eyes towards Jesus, and His divine countenance filled me with courage and consolation. After some travel in this road I emerged into another, differing from it, and far more agreeable. Sweet perfume floated on the air; thick moss formed a soft, green carpet, 'neath which were hid humble violets, whose fragrance only told of their existence. Though I had suffered much in the first road, all sense of pain was gone, and I believed myself near the end of my journey. However, this path led into another, strewn with roses of every color, all bright and full-blown; and this opened into a fourth, broader and lined with white lilies of unequalled loveliness, on leaving which I found myself in the presence of Jesus and Mary. I asked my Jesus where He was while I had been the play of Satan and a prey of horrible thoughts; and He answered: 'I was present in your heart during the combat, and am now myself the reward of your victory.' He told me that virtue is perfected in temptation as gold is purified in the crucible, and that a soul emerges from the fire of tribulation freed from all its miseries. I then saw luscious and beautiful fruits at Mary's feet. Some were of a species unknown to me. The child Jesus took several and gave them to His Mother. She gave me all my apron would hold. Among others, I noticed large pomegranates, and I instantly vowed never to eat another on earth. The Child said to the Blessed Virgin: 'She has now fruits enough for sustenance until her death.' He explained to me that what I had seen were the roads leading first to penance, then humility, succeeded by charity, and, last of all, purity, which led to the vision and possession of God, according to the passage of Scripture: 'Blessed are the pure of heart, for they shall see God.' He then blessed me, and I awoke, my heart filled with ineffable consolations."

CHAPTER VIII.

DEATH OF MADAME CHANAY.

MADAME CHANAY had for many years asked the grace of a happy death. Every Saturday she offered the Blessed Virgin, at her little shrine, a bouquet of most exquisite natural flowers for this intention. As soon as she felt her strength decreasing she resolved to make a general confession, to prepare her soul to meet God; and she sent her younger children away from home, that she might spend some days in quiet retreat. Jane was obliged to go with the others, and she again found herself in the country on the 25th of March, the Feast of the Annunciation, praying for and thinking of her mother. She believed she heard an interior voice telling her to return immediately to the city, where her mother was at the point of death. At first she paid little attention to her premonition; but the voice constantly repeated the command to return to Villefranche, and she was forced to obey. On entering her mother's room she found her engaged in household duties. The mother could not restrain her joy on again seeing her darling, and, tenderly pressing her to her heart, she said: "Now, O Lord! I can die in peace, since I have once more seen my beloved child."

Jane said immediately: "Mother, finish your general confession at once."

"But, my child, my confessor is at Lyons, and will not return until to-morrow."

"In that case I must go for another priest."

On her way she met one of the clergy, whom she asked to come without delay to hear her mother's confession, as she was on the point of death. The priest said he had seen her mother that morning, and found her much better than on the preceding day. Jane's eldest sister confirmed his opinion, and added that she believed her sister was not in her right mind; but she still insisted with so much earnestness that the priest went with her. Madame Chanay asked him to hear her confession, and, after receiving the sacrament, her eyesight dimmed, and in a few moments she could not distinguish the surrounding objects. Extreme Unction was at once administered to her, and, without pain or struggle, she slept in the Lord, on the Feast of the Annunciation, 1813—a day she had always celebrated with the greatest fervor. Her husband had died a few years previous, on the same feast.

Faith softened Jane's sorrow at this event, and gave her the belief that her mother would ere long enjoy in the bosom of the Eternal Father the reward promised her virtue, while the hope of a reunion in heaven was a source of ineffable consolation to her. She sought comfort, too, in prayer, and, prostrating herself at the feet of the Blessed Virgin, she besought her to take the place of the mother she had lost, to watch over her, and direct her thoughts and actions; on her part, she promised Mary to love her more than ever, and to follow faithfully all her inspirations. While her mother's death filled Jane with the greatest affliction, it served to sunder every tie that bound her to earth, and united her more closely to Jesus and Mary.

CHAPTER IX.

MADEMOISELLE CHANAY RESIDES WITH HER SISTER AFTER THE DEATH OF HER MOTHER—HER WORKS OF CHARITY.

AFTER this most trying loss Jane lived a time with her brother-in-law and her eldest sister, Madame Montceni. The great political events entirely turned the scale of fortune in France. The prosperity of the empire was succeeded by the calamities of invasion. A great number of Austrians occupied Villefranche, and many of the officers lodged with the Montceni family. Jane, in her charity, knew no distinction between friend and foe, and all her care and attention were given to the sick and wounded. Her modesty, sweetness, and gentle demeanor won the admiration of all, and they could not dispense with the good Miss, as they named her. Whenever she was missed from the house, they said among themselves: "With God or the sick—either attending the wants of the suffering or in prayer before her God." Every evening she joined them in various innocent amusements, but only on the condition that they would contribute to the poor of the locality. Some time in 1814 she went to reside with her brother at Lyons, and there her time was occupied as it had been at Villefranche. She found means to defray the educational expenses of youth without fortune who had vocation to the priesthood. The wants of the poor touched her inmost heart; she labored day and night for them, and gave abundant alms. Often her zeal carried her beyond the limits of wisdom and prudence. When she heard of young girls giving themselves to disorderly lives, she found no peace until she endeavored to induce them to quit the course they had chosen. She herself went to their dwellings, and forced them to yield to her entreaties by the resistless unction of her words and the influence of her firm will. She never acted on these occasions until after having long and earnestly prayed at the feet of Jesus in the most Blessed Sacrament, and inflicting on herself some corporal penance.

On her rounds of charity she one day discovered a poor family dwelling in a small cabin. Father and mother were prostrated with fever, and five small children stood near the bed clamoring for food. Her heart was all the more saddened at the sight of the misery as she had not the means to relieve their necessities. Quite near was a saloon, whence could be distinctly heard loud revelry and talking. Jane overcame all natural repugnance, and, going at once into the place, she told the men of the condition in which she found the poor family.

After having listened attentively to her, one of the men said: "You ought to be ashamed to beg. 'Tis bad to live in dependence on others, and you are very barefaced in coming here to disturb us with a recital of a well-told and highly-colored story."

She answered with meek gravity: "I gratefully receive what you have said to me as for myself. Please give me something for the wretched family. God will generously reward you."

The man, moved even to tears, took twenty-four francs from his purse, gave them to her, and exhorted the others to follow his example, which all hastened to do; and a sum of two hundred francs was in a few moments obtained for her.

She returned with this to the distressed sufferers, relieved their wants, and left them happy and contented. Jane was doubly gratified in having performed an act of charity, while, at the same time, she gained a victory over self.

CHAPTER X.

HER VOCATION TO THE RELIGIOUS LIFE.

GOD, who never allows Himself to be outdone in generosity, frequently visited His servant with extraordinary graces. One day, being in prayer, her heart, in transports of love, besought Jesus to appear to her. He responded to her petition, and in a vision told her of the union of pure souls with His adorable heart, and of the effort of Satan to prevent this union. Then He made her understand that He wished her heart undivided in its love for Him, and she should have no spouse but Himself. These words filled her soul with joy. Her life was thenceforward that of a soul wounded with love; and, like the dove mentioned in Scripture, she would not rest on earth, but hastened to the shelter of the ark of the religious life. This resolution met with the greatest opposition. Her guardian refused to furnish a dowry; her youngest sister, who was devotedly attached to her, represented that her example was necessary to her salvation; and the devil assailed her with every imaginable temptation. Jane went to Our Lady of Fourvières, a celebrated shrine of the Blessed Virgin, and for nine successive days received Holy Communion there. At the end of the novena she made known all her difficulties to her blessed Mother, and told her that she would not leave the sanctuary without knowing the community she ought to choose and the course she should follow to gain admittance. She remained there several hours on her knees at the foot of the altar, until at last, as though touched by her child-like confidence and persevering prayer, the Blessed Virgin made known to her that she ought to enter the Sisters of St. Joseph, and that she would find at a designated place a person who would furnish the necessary means whereby she could fulfil her pious resolve. She went at once, and found a poor old man, whom she recognized as having frequently seen at Villefranche. He was once possessed of great wealth, but he disposed of it and left all to live in solitude. M. D—— listened graciously to Jane, and showed her into his dwelling, which was poor and meanly furnished. After hearing the account of her mother's death, by which he was moved to tears, he said to Jane:

"Have courage, my child. Your mother was a holy woman, and she will watch over you."

He then conversed with her on the religious state, and promised to speak to the superior of the Sisters of St. Joseph, with whom he was acquainted, and use his influence to gain her admittance into the congregation, and, if necessary, furnish her with a complete outfit and pay her dowry.

Jane returned to the city full of joy. Her friends were anxiously awaiting her, as they could not account for her absence and delay. Her brother demanded, with much severity, where she had been all the morning. She told him she was in search of the father and benefactor among strangers that she could not find in her own family, and had found a patron who would furnish her with means to enter a religious house. Her brother was much angered, and said he would oppose her carrying out her design, as she was not yet of age; but her sister, Madame Montceni, who had charge of all the children, interfered, and persuaded the brother to accede to Jane's desire. Consequently, after a few days she entered the convent of the Sisters of St. Joseph, established at Lyons, on old St. Peter Street.

CHAPTER XI.

ORIGIN OF SISTERS OF ST. JOSEPH—ESTABLISHED AT PUY 1650—GROWTH OF INSTITUTE—DISPERSION OF SISTERS, 1790—THEIR RE-ESTABLISHMENT IN THE DIOCESE OF LYONS, 1807.

THE foundation of the Sisters of St. Joseph dates back to the first half of the seventeenth century. In establishing the order of the Visitation St. Francis de Sales entertained the desire to found a congregation of women joining to the ordinary exercises of the religious life visits to the sick and the poor, and to serve in every way to promote the comfort and salvation of their neighbors. This plan, fully carried out during the first years of the institution of 1612, was in a short time modified at the request of M. de Marquemonte, Archbishop of Lyons, who considered enclosure as essential to the stability of the edifice. St. Francis de Sales, on the contrary, wished to join the life of Martha with that of Mary—the external works of charity and mercy to those of rest and contemplation; in a word, the active with the contemplative.

"My design," he said, "was to unite these two so intimately that they would render mutual aid, the one assisting the other, and that the Sisters, in working for their own sanctification, would at the same time relieve the wants of their neighbors and labor for their salvation. To enjoin enclosure at present would be to destroy an essential part of the institution, deprive their neighbor of necessary aid and good example, and deprive the Sisters themselves of the merit of the works of charity recommended in the Gospel and authorized by the example of our divine Lord."

In spite of the force of these reasonings, St. Francis de Sales yielded his judgment, and enclosure became a part of the constitutions of the Visitation approved by Pope Paul V. in 1618. In speaking of this change the Bishop of Geneva was wont to say:

"People call me the founder of the Visitation; is anything more unreasonable? I have undone what I wished to do, and I did what I wished not to do."

The design of a mind so great as St. Francis de Sales' responded too well to the growing wants of society to have it die with him. On the contrary, we see, a few years after his death, spring up in all parts communities of women devoted to the relief of human miseries, and accomplishing external works of charity, thereby adding a new gem to the brilliant crown of the religious life. Many of these were placed under the patronage of St. Joseph, but the Sisters of Puy were established with the particular view of realizing the first design of St. Francis de Sales, which was renewed in the mind of a pious missionary of the Society of Jesus, John Peter Medaille, who had labored with great fruit in the dioceses of Puy, Clermont, Saint Flour, Rhodes, and Vienna.

This good father having, in the course of his missions, met with several widows and pious young women who were desirous to retire from the world and devote themselves to the service of the salvation of their neighbor, but were deterred for want of means to enter convents, he formed the intention to propose to some bishop the establishment of a congregation into which those devoted women could enter and devote themselves to labor for their salvation, and fulfil all the good works of which they were capable in the service of their neighbor. He made known this wish to Monseigneur de Maupas, Bishop of Puy. This prelate, who entertained a particular veneration for St. Francis de Sales' memory and wrote his life, received the offer with joy. He assembled the subjects prepared by Father Medaille at Puy, and lodged them for some time with a pious lady in the city named Lucretia de Blanche, wife of Mr. Joux, a gentleman of Sance, who labored until her death with an extraordinary charity and zeal for the advancement of their congregation. Bishop Maupas placed them in charge of an orphan asylum at Puy, where, on the 15th of October (Feast of St. Teresa), 1650, he established them and placed them under the protection of St. Joseph. A short time after he gave them another asylum at Montferrand and directed them to educate the orphans kindly received there; and on the 10th of

March, 1651, he gave them letters for the regular founding of a congregation under the title of Daughters of St. Joseph. In the rules formed on this occasion the pious bishop recommended his dear daughters to the goodness of his brother bishops.

"My lords," he said, "are most humbly and earnestly requested to have paternal charity and particular care to maintain and advance this little congregation, in consideration of the great St. Francis de Sales, since it has been established to revive the spirit of the first institution that this prelate made of the Sisters of the Visitation."

The first chapter of their constitutions says:

"In all their conduct the Sisters should endeavor to follow the style of dress, the spirit, and the life of the Daughters of the Visitation, and should have a special regard for their holy founder and for all the religious of the order, and do all in their power to retain the spirit with which St. Francis de Sales had inspired them."

The name Sisters of St. Joseph he explains in these terms:

"They bear the name 'Congregation of

St. Joseph,' that the Sisters composing it, in imitation of their glorious patron, may serve their neighbor with the same care, charity, diligence, and cordiality that animated St. Joseph in serving Mary, his most chaste spouse, and her divine Son Jesus."

Monseigneur Armand de Bethune, who succeeded Henry Maupas as Bishop of Puy, confirmed the congregation and its rules by letters of approbation on the 23d of September, 1665. Louis XIV. gave letters-patent in 1666 in approval of the first establishment at Puy, St. Didier, and many other places of Vellay. In 1693 houses of the congregation were founded in the dioceses of Clermont, Vienne, Lyons, Grenoble, Embrun, Gap, Viviers, and many others. Henry Villars, Archbishop of Vienne, who had established them in the great Hôtel Dieu of that city in 1668, approved their institute by letters on the 2d of that year, and ordered a printed edition of their rules, which until that time existed only in manuscript.

In 1729 the Sisters of St. Joseph in the Diocese of Lyons became so numerous as to necessitate a new edition of the constitutions, which received the approbation of Francis Paul Neuville Villeroy, Archbishop of Lyons, on the 20th of December the same year.

The revolution in 1790 blighted the growing congregation and dispersed all the communities of the Sisters of St. Joseph. The most flourishing of these at the time was that of Manistrol, placed under the direction of Mother St. John, who had been brought up under the protective shelter of the convent, and had succeeded her aunt in the office of superior at the early age of twenty-five years. This good religious refused to take the required oath of allegiance, in the name of all the Sisters, saying, "The head answers for the body." She was thrown into prison with Sisters St. Teresa and St. Martha, and there patiently awaited the summons to the guillotine. She had paid her last sous for having their habits repaired, that they might appear with becoming decency before the public, when the fall of Robespierre gave them liberty. On receiving the news she turned towards her Sisters, and in tones full of sadness said to them:

"We were not worthy to die in the cause

of religion; our sins were an obstacle to the reception of this signal favor."

She went to reside with her father, until the letter addressed to the religious of Puy by their bishop, Gallard, who had fled to Switzerland, recalled them to their works and exercises. After the restoration of freedom of religious principles and worship in France, many of the old religious of St. Joseph and some young persons assembled at St. Stephen's to live in community, according to the advice of Monseigneur Cholleton, curé of that city. This venerable priest invited Mother St. John to take the direction of this community, with which request she complied on the 14th of August, 1807. In the following year Cardinal Fesch, Archbishop of Lyons, and M. Bochard, his vicar-general, struck with the great good produced by the re-establishment of the Sisters of St. Joseph, gave their attention to them, and allowed them to resume the religious habit and receive professions. The authorization of the state was obtained April 10, 1812, and the diocese soon numbered several flourishing communities, among which was distinguished the house of Lyons, situated on the old St. Peter Street, and under the direction of Sister St. Paul. It was into this establishment that Jane Chanay sought admittance and was received.

CHAPTER XII.

HER NOVITIATE.

MADEMOISELLE CHANAY experienced a sensible joy on her entrance into the novitiate, and the Sisters of St. Joseph were not less happy in receiving her. Her reputation had preceded her into the community, and even the first day after her admission her profound humility, fidelity to rule, charity towards her neighbor, her joy, her spirit of obedience, but, above all, her ardent love of God, were manifest to all. The sister-portress often told that all her companions entertained a great respect for the young postulant, and that, besides the religious virtues of which she gave the example, they could perceive most extraordinary gifts, such as frequent ecstasies and a discernment of spirits. It was universally thought she could read the secrets of one's soul; and so firm was this belief in the minds of the young Sisters that they would sometimes hide themselves on her approach, lest she would penetrate their thoughts. Her humility and obedience were her safeguard. She believed herself the most miserable of creatures; the faults of her life were constantly present in her mind, and in a spirit of most profound abasement she imagined herself at the foot of the cross. Accustomed from her infancy to extraordinary favors, she did not wonder at their possession, but imagined she shared them in common with all Christian souls. Almost every day some new marvel was learned concerning her, and they soon regarded her as a saint. One day she received news of the serious illness of her sister, Madame Montceni, and immediately asked permission to make a novena at Fourvières. One of the religious asked her if she hoped her sister would recover.

She replied: "I believe she will be restored to health as firmly as that I am here The Blessed Virgin will not refuse my petition." Two weeks from that day, and without knowing the result of the novena, on hearing the door-bell ring, she said to the sister-portress, to whom she was speaking: "That is my sister"; and her saying proved true. Seven weeks were sufficient to convince her superiors that Mademoiselle Chanay was truly called by God. She received the religious habit and commenced her novitiate on the 3d of January, 1815. Her director, M. Laurette, preached the sermon customary on such occasions, and congratulated the Sisters on receiving among them a soul so privileged. The eve of her retreat preparatory to her reception, Jane went to purchase the necessaries for the feast which was to be celebrated in honor of her reception.

She greatly regretted using the money in this way that she wished to give to the poor, and, under the impulse of this thought, she took from her purse two sous and gave them to a poor woman, unperceived by the Sister who accompanied her. She very soon experienced most lively regret for having disposed of this sum without permission. Above all, she dared not acknowledge her fault to her superior, and she had recourse to Mary, and said to her with simple confidence: "Give me back the two sous,

Mother, and I promise you the lesson will benefit me, and I will never again dispose of anything without permission."

Mary heard her favorably; for a few days afterwards the young postulant met on the steps of the house a poor woman with a little child. She asked her how she came there, adding that she had not a sou, and could give her nothing. The woman replied:

"Mademoiselle, it was to me you gave two sous on the street a few days ago, and I have come to return them to you."

Jane received them with joy, and hastened to give them to the superior, acknowledging at the same time her fault, and related what had happened. Mother St. Paul treasured these two sous as a relic, and still had them a few years previous to her death.

Shortly before receiving the holy habit Jane prayed with great fervor that she might receive the name of St. Joseph, as she always had great confidence in him. She manifested her desire to the superior, who said:

"It is too late; the names are selected."

"Mother," pleaded Jane, "bandage my

eyes; let me draw in the 'Lives of the Saints'; and if I draw the name St. Joseph, won't you give it to me?"

The superior smiled at the simplicity of the child, and acceded to her request. The pin marked St. Joseph; and this circumstance greatly added to the joy that animated every faculty of Jane's soul on divesting herself for ever of her worldly garb.

CHAPTER XIII.

SISTER ST. JOSEPH AT CHAZAY.

IMMEDIATELY after having received the habit, M. Bochard, who entertained great expectations of the "little Sister St. Joseph," wished to send her to Chazay-ou-Ain, one of the parishes in his diocese. The priests there were frequently subjected to gross insults, and many of the people made open profession of infidelity. Sister St. Joseph had for superior a person inclined to rather too great severity, and well calculated to exercise the virtue of her Sisters. Her commands were rather those of the autocrat than the religious superior, and their fulfilment met with little approval from her. This, however, did not deter Sister St. Joseph from manifesting great respect towards her. God rewarded this conduct on the part of the young novice by inspiring the superior to give her the advice most useful for her, whenever she rendered an account of the state of her conscience. Direction was at that time all the more necessary for her, as she was constantly tormented by a desire to enter a cloistered order; but this desire was overruled by her spirit of obedience. She also wished to become a lay Sister, so as to avoid the possibility of ever being charged with the responsibility of others. For a long time she earnestly prayed for this purpose. She was given many of the duties of a lay Sister. While directing several classes, she had also to attend to cooking, baking, and other works beyond her strength; for her constitution was weak and delicate. On the arrival of the Sisters the house was almost a ruin, having neither doors nor windows, so that the closing of the house at night was only effected by the ingenious devices of the Sisters. No comfort of any description was afforded them. They slept on mattresses on the floor, and were content with scant covering. The city itself had, at the time, little or no resources. The poor, numerous at all times, were increased by the famine of 1816. In order to relieve their miseries the Sisters worked day and night to obtain and distribute alms to the poor. Sister St. Joseph, in particular, imposed on herself the most difficult privations, and exercised all her activity and invention to supply resources for the new foundation. Through the influence of her relations at Lyons and Villefranche, several young girls were sent to Chazay to receive an education, and soon an academy was opened, which considerably improved the condition of the community. The Sisters also visited the sick, and were lavish in the care and devotion bestowed on them. A poor woman afflicted with cancer was entrusted to Sister St. Joseph. For her unremitting care and attention she received only murmurs and ingratitude from her patient.

M. Bochard closely observed all the good works accomplished by his spiritual children, took great interest in the increasing prosperity of the community of Chazay and the great good effected there by Sister St. Joseph. As soon as the two years of her novitiate were completed, he delegated M. Papillon, curé of the parish, to receive the vows of the young novice, which ceremony took place the 3d of January, 1817, in the church of Chazay.

The fervor of her novitiate tells with what sentiments Sister St. Joseph pronounced her vows. She called the day of her profession the happiest of her life. Before she was but the betrothed; she was now the bride, and her love for Jesus increased every moment.

At this time the government of the Sisters of St. Joseph underwent a marked change. Before the Revolution, and in the few years succeeding, each community was in itself independent. Unity of origin and the spirit of the rules maintained the links of charity, and all formed but one family; but each house had its absolute superior, who gave the habit and received professions. In 1812 the difficulties and the wants of the times, the great number of houses composed of only two or three religious, made manifest the necessity for the establishment of a general novitiate, where there could be assembled all that was necessary to the proper and effective formation of subjects. With this purpose M. Bochard bought the old convent of Chartreux at Lyons, which, in 1816, was made the principal mother-house of the congregation and the residence of a superior charged, by special decision of the ordinary, with the general administration of the order and the placing of all the Sisters. Mother St. John was destined to fill this important position, and with the aid of M. Bochard she established numerous houses of the congregation. In 1817 the new superior-general sent Sister St. Regis to direct the establishment at Chazay. This house, composed of five or six religious, conducted a numerously-attended academy. Sister St. Joseph continually attracted souls by her virtues and her indefatigable zeal. The catechism class, with which she was charged, afforded her an occasion, which she eagerly embraced, to speak of God, His love and His perfections. She soon added to her class for children one for grown persons, and acquitted herself with such success that every week hundreds from Chazay and the neighboring parishes flocked to hear her instructions and explanation of Christian truths. The Sunday dances, which were continued late in the night, together with the ignorance of even the principles of religion, were a great obstacle to the good of the parish. Sister St. Joseph devised a strange means to put a stop to these. One day, after catechism, she detained some of the young girls who were in a hurry to leave the convent, and told them she wanted to go to the dance-house with them. The wild young girls needed no second request. She accompanied them, and, after observing their manner, complimented them on their graceful motions, but added: "Chazay could be renowned for its dancers if a few lessons on the principles of dancing were given. I will instruct you free of charge if you attend in great numbers."

The news was quickly spread throughout the city, and on the following day forty young girls came for instruction. During the week the Sister practised them assiduously, and on the succeeding Sunday her pupils were the admiration of all. The second week her class was still more numerous; but this time she spoke to them of the vanity and nothingness of earthly joys, and of the great beauty, fulness, and truth of religious practices, with such ardor and zeal that many of them eschewed their Sunday amusements, and some embraced the religious life. She exercised so great control over the people of Chazay that several times she went to the places of amusement, took the violin from the hands of the performer, broke the strings, and forced all the young girls to leave. They murmured at this act after she had gone, but dared say nothing in her presence.

Her health soon began to fail, and she was subject to frequent attacks of illness; nevertheless, she continued her labors, and, while enduring intense pain, managed to hide her sufferings. An unusually pleasant manner and amiability were the means she used to hide the sufferings that racked an overtaxed constitution. Divine Providence frequently rewarded her generosity with the most affectionate care. Once, when even the sight of food excited nausea, the superior pressed her to mention anything she thought would be palatable. She asked for a bird, and, on being told that none could be procured, she requested the superior to open the window and give her what would enter. The Mother complied, and a bird flew in.

which was prepared for the invalid, who ate it with relish.

Sisters' presence at recreation was a source of enlivening joy, so much so that on Thursday of every week the religious from the neighboring houses came to spend the day at Chazay. At one of these reunions, in speaking of the establishment then projected at Belley, and surmising what Sisters were to be sent there, she arose and said: "Sisters! hail the new superior of Belley."

They enjoyed the saying, but she gravely added: "Yes, superior of Belley, afterwards of Gap, and later of Bordeaux. I shall die near the sea."

Sister St. Paul, who accompanied her to Bordeaux, was then a boarder at Chazay, and often related this prediction, which, at the time, seemed unlikely to attain its fulfilment. Monseigneur Devie, a short time after this, recalled her to Lyons, and told her she was destined to go to Belley and found a house there, adding: "You must be ready to receive great opposition and many contradictions; for no one there wants the Sisters of St. Joseph." She objected, on account of her youth, ignorance, and want of capacity, to assume so great a responsibility. The venerable old man, having a prospective view of all the good to be accomplished by her energy and her influence, raised his cane over her, and smilingly said: "Obey, and leave immediately."

CHAPTER XIV.

HER WORKS AT BELLEY.

MOTHER ST. JOSEPH was sent to Belley in 1819, being then in her twenty-fourth year. Sister St. Thomas, who was twelve years her senior, accompanied her. A religious community of another order had already been established there, and the Sisters of St. Joseph were not desired. The parish priest at the cathedral, M. Guillomot, a relative of M. Bochard, was opposed to the wish of the vicar-general to establish the Sisters there. The first visit of the young superior was made to M. Guillomot, who saluted her with "What do you want here, little Sister?"

"I am here through obedience, and am happy that my lot sends me to you, in whom I can find a counsellor, father, and friend."

"Your speech is very flattering; but I

must tell you I am not pleased to have you come here. The authorities should have consulted me before imposing religious on me. I tell you sincerely that all the people are against you, and you will get no assistance in the city. The children will not be sent to your schools, for all our wants in educational facilities are already supplied by the religious already established here. I advise you to return at once to Lyons."

This reception would have disconcerted any other than Mother St. Joseph. She, however, replied that she knew he would be all she could wish to her new foundation—zealous friend, a tender father, and a devoted protector. Frequently, during the ten years following he asked pardon for his discouraging remarks, and thanked Providence for the gift forced on him. On leaving the pastor's house they repaired to that of Madame Beatrix, a wealthy and pious lady, to whom M. Bochard had written letters of introduction. She gave them a still colder welcome than the priest, but consented to allow them to remain with her a short time. After a week the prejudice of M. Guillomot softened on his becoming better acquainted with the virtues of the young foundress, and he gave her the use of a small house near the presbytery, where she soon assembled over one hundred children. Notwithstanding the labor attendant on the number of their pupils, the two Sisters daily visited the poor, the prisoners, and the sick. Mother St. Joseph gave them all at her disposal. M. Guillomot, perceiving how she imposed privations on herself, without her knowledge replaced the objects given away; but the new gifts were distributed as soon as received. The priest then lent what he deemed necessary for the house, in order that the Mother might not dispose of what she had only the storage. Sister St. Thomas, on her part, wished to limit the excessive charity of her superior. They agreed that the silver coin given in payment for tuition should be used for the house, and the currency expended or the wants of the poor. But charity is ever ingenious. Mother St. Joseph requested the pupils to make their payments in currency, and thus the greater part of the community resources continued to be applied to the relief of the distressed.

A few months sufficed for the people to learn appreciation of Mother St. Joseph's worth and dispel their prejudices. Opposition vanished as by enchantment. M. Bochard, hearing of her success, judged it time to open a novitiate, and he communicated his design to her. She readily acceded to his wishes. Even on the day of its opening several postulants presented themselves to be received, and the house provided by M. Guillomot was soon found inadequate to accommodate those who sought admission. On the other hand, the works of charity performed by the Sisters were spoken of among the ladies of the city. These resolved to concentrate their labors, and, under the direction of the Sisters, to organize a house whence daily distributions of soup, clothing, and fuel could be made. This measure obliged Mother St. Joseph to look for a building suitable for the purpose. In this instance, as was her wont, she had recourse to God, and in the ardor of her prayer she believed she heard our Lord tell her to purchase a chapter-house. She said aloud: "And where are the means, Lord? If you wish me to obey your inspiration, I beg you to show the way, and I will follow." Although she possessed but thirty francs, which Sister St. Thomas had managed to keep from her, she offered a considerable sum for a property she learned was for sale. It was a spacious building, with extensive grounds, but the interior was in need of great repairs. These many difficulties did not dampen her energies nor force her to desist from her purpose. Accustomed to place herself entirely under the care of divine Providence, she worked on and always found means to attain the end. Many obstacles were put in her way; nevertheless, the bargain was concluded, and payments postponed until the minors of the family to whom the building belonged had attained majority, thus enabling the Sisters to begin the work. The necessary repairs called for lumber to the value of three thousand francs, and the sanguine superior purchased the quantity from a neighboring merchant, with a promise of payment on delivery. Workmen were engaged and the project begun without delay.

CHAPTER XV.

HER SPIRIT OF POVERTY AND GREAT CONFIDENCE IN DIVINE PROVIDENCE.

ON ner return to the convent, and while giving thanks to God for His favors in the enterprise, she was seized with a general debility, and on the following day had high fever and delirium. The physicians ordered the necessary remedies, never even suspecting that the Sisters had not the means to purchase them. Sister St. Thomas wished to borrow money for the medicines, but the superior would not listen to the proposal, and said: "I have all I want." The illness increased, and on the seventh day the patient received the last sacraments. The physician, surprised at the unfavorable effects of the remedies, enquired if the prescriptions were carefully followed. An answer in the negative was scarcely necessary, for a moment's observation showed him they were not. This culpable negligence drew from him a severe rebuke to the patient and the Sisters. When one medicine after another was ordered, and after long delay not found forthcoming, the true state of the case dawned upon him, and he immediately, from his own purse, had the orders filled. By his unstinted praises on every occasion he showed himself an admirer of Sister St. Joseph. M. Guillomot ever afterwards anticipated the wants of the Sisters. His confidence in Mother St. Joseph was unlimited, and this, in return, was reciprocated by her. He prayed incessantly, and obliged the obedient religious to ask God to restore her to health. Nevertheless, every sign of approaching death was indicated, when M. l'Abbé Duluy advised her to make a vow to go to the Indies, if obedience permitted. Her confessor eagerly seized on this last hope of rescuing her from death. She obeyed, and immediately the fever left her; little by little her strength returned, and she again resumed her duties of labor and devotion. In the meantime the proprietor of the lumber-yard had asked payment for his lumber. The superior had promised to pay him in eight days. She had nothing, but prayed to God with her wonted confidence and eagerness to inspire some persons, whom He would tell her of, to aid her in her extremity. She tried every means to obtain it, but without success. "Lord," she said, "there are now but a few hours before payment will be required. What confusion for your spouse to break her word! The discredit is as much to you as to me; for persons know it was in your name I acted." In a little while, with the simplicity of a child, she said: "A woman in the world needs not be uneasy about the administration of affairs, for her spouse attends to them. You are my spouse, Lord; do, then, what I wish." These petitions of love and confidence were accompanied by many privations; even indulgences of the most innocent kind, and which were advised her for her health, were abandoned. The hour for payment did not bring the required amount. She went to the chapel, and, taking up a New Testament, she opened at the passage in which St. John writes: "Verily, verily I say unto you, all you ask the Father in my name shall be given you."

"Lord," she said, "you yourself have inspired these words. I ask you to keep your promise." After praying a few moments on her knees, and not receiving a response, she went behind the altar and knocked on the door of the tabernacle, saying: "No answer yet, Lord. I want three thousand francs without delay." Frightened at her seeming want of reverence, she left the chapel and proceeded to her room. On entering she perceived on the floor a handkerchief containing six-franc pieces. On counting them she found the exact sum necessary to meet the lumber-bill and house repairs.

As soon as the religious were settled in their new house the departments for the several supplies needed for the relief of the poor and afflicted were stored by the charitable superior, and distributions daily made. Her great activity enabled her to supply all, and her ardent charity was like a fire, warming all hearts and filling them with mercy and love towards the poor. She harbored a desire to establish an orphan asylum and home for the aged, but was forced, for want of means, to defer the execution of her good design until a later period. The work undertaken with greatest courage, at the command of her superior and the dictates of her own heart, was the founding of a novitiate. Several postulants waited with a holy impatience to be classed in the number of her daughters. It was a source of great joy to her to see their young souls animated with love for God, and, when she could, she infused into them some of the fire that burned in her own soul. She loved them with the tender love of a devoted mother, but always expected an absolute obedience and a spirit of poverty and mortification. The vivacity of her character sometimes carried her too far; but her charity made up for all. She possessed the gift of subduing the most incorrigible. The tenderness of her heart tempered the energy of her nature, and she knew how to render possible, though not always agreeable, acts most painful to nature in the fulfilment of religious obedience. Several novices and sixteen postulants had been received into the novitiate, when the re-establishment of the Diocese of Belley, in 1823, brought about a change in the government of the Sisters of St. Joseph.

CHAPTER XVI.

MONSEIGNEUR DEVIE NOMINATED BISHOP OF BELLEY—MOTHER ST. JOSEPH APPOINTED SUPERIOR-GENERAL OF THE SISTERS OF ST. JOSEPH.

MGR. Alexander Raymond Devie, Vicar-General of Valence, was promoted to the bishopric of Belley on February 13, 1823, consecrated on June 15, and inaugurated July 23 of the same year. This prelate, one of the greatest of his time, soon perceived that a great amount of good might be effected by the Sisters of St. Joseph, and he resolved to give their labors a new and beneficial impulse. Outside the novitiate at Belley the Sisters had a number of houses in the diocese. The new bishop obtained leave to have them independent of Lyons, and to form a congregation, for which he proposed Mother St. Joseph as superior-general. Claimed at the same time by the superiors at Lyons, on account of having been received into the congregation there, and by Mons. Devie, as useful in carrying out his project, she decided on returning to Lyons, and was on her way there, when the carriage that conveyed her met with an accident a short distance from Belley, and prevented a continuance of the journey. Mons. Devie, accepting this mishap as an omen in his favor, sent orders for her return; the superior at Lyons gave the required convent, and the young religious was given the office of Superior-General of the Congregation.

About this time she had an extraordinary dream, which remained indelibly stamped on her memory all her life, and inspired her with great dread of God's judgment. For many years succeeding her mother's death prayers for the repose of her soul were offered by her devoted daughter; but, owing to her great confidence in the mercy of God and her knowledge of her mother's virtue, for some time past she had omitted prayers for her. One night, while in a deep sleep, she thought she saw her mother near her bed, and, on expressing joy at seeing her, the mother said reproachfully: "My dear daughter, I am still in the fire of purgatory." Mother St. Joseph asked how it was possible that one so devoted to the poor and so pious could be there, deprived of the vision of God and the reward of her good works. Instead of answering her, the mother touched her arm with the tip of her finger, and Mother St. Joseph withdrew it immediately, as if a red-hot iron had been applied. Madame Chanay then said: "You cannot endure in even one spot the fire to which my whole existence is subjected." She told her the cause of her detention in purgatory, and exacted a promise from her of prayers for her deliverance. The vision vanished, and Mother St. Joseph awoke, struck with a lively impression of what she had seen and heard. The most extraordinary feature of the dream was that the part the mother touched left a wound, which caused intense pain. The physician could not understand its origin, and he applied various remedies, but without effect. The wound was open for a long time, the arm always retained a weakness, and the scar of the burned place remained until death. Sometimes Mother St. Joseph showed it to the Sister who slept in the room with her, and said: "If I suffer so much from so slight an evil, what would it be to be plunged for ever into eternal fire?"

The duties of her new charge, far from lessening, seemed to increase her ardor in performing works of mercy and her desire for the salvation of souls.

She profited by the confidence which the poor placed in her to draw them to God. She showed them the goodness of our Lord in sending relief and comfort to the needy and distressed, and how blamable are those who neglect to pray to Him and obey His laws; for the charity they received was sent by Him whom they feared not to outrage. Her persuasive words, accompanied by acts of the most sacrificing and generous devotion, disposed them to consider their faults, and a great number of those she assisted became good and fervent Christians. God favored her also with the special light and grace of discernment of the state of souls. Many instances are related, the recital of which would be of no small interest to the reader; but it is deemed sufficient to say that this gift, usually accorded to those through whom God effects good to fellow-creatures, was hers in a remarkable degree.

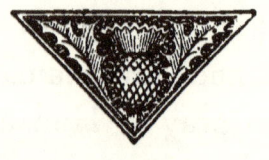

CHAPTER XVII.

DIFFICULTIES EXPERIENCED BY MOTHER ST. JOSEPH IN HER ADMINISTRATION—FOUNDING OF DIVERS INDUSTRIAL SCHOOLS AT BELLEY.

IN the administration of Mother St Joseph as superior-general she soon experienced difficulties opposed to a character like hers, as lively as it was firm, and to the nature of her mind, as prompt to execute as to conceive, though she was accustomed always to count on extraordinary interpositions of divine Providence when ordinary means failed. The greater number of the sisters were older than the superior-general, and, not having been formed under her direction, many of them disapproved of her mode of action; moreover, her health was fast failing. All these circumstances convinced her that God would not long require her to hold the position in the congregation, and she undertook to bring about the election of a new superior-general. The event took place at Belley in July, 1824, during a retreat, at which were assembled one hundred and twenty-seven religious. Many among them wished to re-elect Mother St. Joseph, but she firmly manifested a decided intention to relinquish the charge, and she effectively directed the votes of the Sisters for Mother St. Benedict, who was unanimously elected. In the same retreat Mother St. Joseph was nominated assistant-general of the Congregation.

Immediately after this Mgr. Devie resolved to remove the mother-house and novitiate of the Sisters to the city of Bourg, the most central point in his diocese. As assistant, Mother St. Joseph should have accompanied Mother Benedict, but the bishop wished her to remain at Belley and consolidate the works she had commenced. Relieved of the burden of the general administration, she applied herself above all to cultivate to perfection at Belley the interior life, an exemplary regularity, and provide every facility for the thorough education of the young girls with whom the Sisters were charged.

These cares, however, could not absorb the superabundant charity and zeal with which God had blessed her. Every misery found an echo in her sympathetic soul; and when she herself had not means to relieve the afflicted, she applied to Him to whom all things are possible.

On her arrival at Belley, in 1819, she was struck by the misery and indolence of the people. Accustomed from her youth to a life of labor, she had a horror of idleness, and was grieved to see robust men, as well as women and children, begging in the streets. She knew by experience that the first means toward ameliorating the wretchedness of a population is to inspire a taste for industry, love of order, and economy; therefore she tried to introduce into the country industrial schools for women and children. Some houses in Lyons sent her straw material to have made into hats. This trade had been introduced into Chazay by her, but want of aptitude in the people of Belley rendered her project there futile. She accordingly established a manufactory of rings made of horse-hair and beads, which continued during many years to give occupation to a number of persons. She tried to organize sewing-schools on a large scale, but this brought too small profit to attract many workers. A new thought came to her relief. She remembered in her youth to have raised silk-worms, and the thought was a flash of light to her. She went immediately into the country around Belley to look for mulberry-trees for her purpose. As soon as practicable she got grain, and engaged several women to aid her in the work. For fear they would become discouraged, she let them work during the day, reserving the night-work for herself. Good wages were offered to those willing to engage themselves. Soon the desire of great gain without much fatigue induced persons to come from all parts to ask instruction from the mother. A great number of mulberry-trees were planted, and in a few years the country was rich in an industry that gave occupation to a great number of families until then victims of misery and idleness. Mother St. Joseph always retained a tender regard for the silk-worms, which she called the instruments of divine Providence. She raised a few every year, and appropriated their produce to works of charity. About this time her zeal for the salvation of souls was the occasion of placing her life in peril. She had rescued two young girls from ruin, and placed them in a secure refuge. Their destroyer conceived so great a hatred for her that he threatened to take her life at the first opportunity. One night, as she was returning from a visit to the sick poor, accompanied by only one Sister, he threw at her from a great height a large block, which, by a visible interposition of divine Providence, fell at her feet without doing her any injury. This man continued his threats and annoyances until the bishop deemed it necessary to send Mother St. Joseph away for a time.

CHAPTER XVIII.

FOUNDATION OF THE HOUSE AT FERNEY.

ONE of the principal cares of Bishop Devie was to guard his flock against the influence of Protestants, who, in the neighborhood of Geneva, were especially aggressive. On his first pastoral visit to Ferney, in 1823, he found the Calvinistic principles were rooted there. This small city, which was on the extreme frontier and facing Geneva, was, under the Restoration, the rendezvous for the infidel minds of Europe who had flocked to strengthen themselves in the worship of Voltaire. The Protestants, though few in number, owned the greater part of the property, and they obtained permission from the government to build a temple of worship, to which they endeavored to attract Catholics. These had no school, and their little parish church could not accommodate one-fourth of the congregation.

The pious bishop was deeply touched at the critical state of affairs, and he resolved to build a large church and establish schools there. The church was finished in November, 1826. In the interval Mother St. Joseph was called from Belley by Mgr. Devie, who, knowing the fervor of her devotion and her great spirit of sacrifice, sent her to Ferney to found a house of her order.

The obedient religious left Belley, accompanied by Sister Wilfrid and another Sister, and went at once to the presbytery. The parish priest was an aged man, and but little disposed to incur the expense of furnishing a house for the Sisters. A custom at that time existed of giving the pastor the winding-sheets used for the dead. These were laid aside without being washed, and kept until charity called for them. Mother St. Joseph and her companions were on this occasion given them for use; and as the religious knew by experience that the renunciation of self-love attracted the blessing of God on their works, in spite of their repugnance, they made no complaint and used the sheets. Mother St. Joseph afterwards assured her daughters that the nights passed in this penance were for her times of grace and spiritual favors. While Mother St. Joseph lived at Ferney her youngest sister, being threatened with total blindness, wrote to her, saying she depended on her prayers to avert the evil. She advised her to make a pilgrimage to a certain shrine of the Blessed Virgin, and pray there, assuring her that many prayers should be offered for the intention of her recovery. The girl did as she was directed, and was blessed with perfect restoration to sight.

The house at Ferney was in a few months established on a solid foundation, and Mother St. Joseph had commenced all that Mgr. Devie expected from her zeal, when Providence interrupted the course of her apostolate.

Her health gave way on account of her excessive labors and the rigorous penances to which she subjected herself Inflammation of the lungs set in, and in a few days made great ravages. Frequent hemorrhages excited the alarm of all except the patient, who looked for nothing but that the will of God be absolutely accomplished in her. The physicians of Geneva said that death was inevitable, and her family came to demand leave for her to enjoy the benefit of her native air.

Before leaving, she wished to consult a particular doctor. On his entrance into her room, she said:

"Doctor, is there any hope of my recovery?"

"Sister, youth is in your favor. Your case is not hopeless; but it may take a long time for your recovery."

She replied: "Doctor, you are not addressing a worldling. Remember, I entered religion to learn to die well. Tell me, as a friend, what you think of my state."

These solicitations forced the doctor to say: "I do not believe you can recover. If the hemorrhages cease, it is possible for you to live three weeks."

She thanked the doctor for his information, and assured him of her prayers. In the conviction that she would die in a few days, she refused to go to her family, and asked to return to Belley to breathe her last with her daughters. The journey was so fatiguing, and her physical prostration so great, that the attendants several times supposed her dying.

CHAPTER XIX.

HER RECOVERY ON ST. ANTHELME'S DAY—FAVORS OBTAINED BY HER PRAYERS.

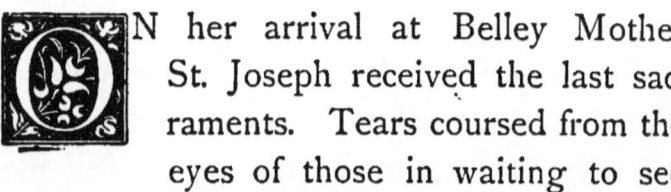N her arrival at Belley Mother St. Joseph received the last sacraments. Tears coursed from the eyes of those in waiting to see die, from one moment to another, her whom they called the mother of the poor and of the afflicted. Mgr. Devie visited her frequently and shared in the general sadness.

One day she felt an extreme faintness, and she believed her last hour had come. It was a time of grace. The Infant Jesus appeared to her, and filled her soul with a great joy.

"Come," He said, "and see what I have prepared for those that fear me."

"Lord, I love you more than I fear you."

The divine Child showed her a magnificent palace, the walls of which were studded with precious stones brighter than the sun; and in showing her through He seemed pleased with her astonishment and admiration. When the door opened, she was dazzled by the transcendent splendor manifest, and Jesus showed her a seat of surpassing beauty which He had prepared for her in the assembly of the saints. She believed the time had come for her to rest there; but He said: "Behold! and may the light which is shown you direct you through the darkness in which you must remain."

The Child asked her in what manner she wished to be cured. She requested that the glory of her recovery be attributed to St. Anthelme, patron of the city and the diocese, whose feast was to be celebrated in a few days. The vision disappeared, and the patient opened her eyes without any apparent improvement in her state of health, but in her heart had a certainty of her recovery. The following day she made known to Mgr. Devie all that passed. She exacted a promise from Father Colletta to clothe a certain number of poor persons if she recovered on St. Anthelme's day. It was usual for Mass to be celebrated in the chapel of the saint at midnight on the feast, and she asked the doctor to allow her to assist at the Mass, assuring him that she would recover.

"Yes," replied the doctor, "recover from all ills. You will die before that time."

"Cure me, then, with the aid of medicine," she said.

He was much annoyed at her persistence, and said: "You know I would do all in my power to cure you."

"But if I recover, what will you do?"

"I will be fully converted, heart and soul."

On leaving, he gave orders to the Sisters not to accede to her request, and that she might be kept a few days longer with them. When the hour neared, she renewed her importunities, and the Sisters went to consult Mgr. Devie, who was walking near his house, viewing the illumination of the city. Knowing what was promised his spiritual daughter, he replied: "Do whatever she wishes."

The bishop went himself to the shrine of the saint when the patient, as pale as a corpse, was brought in. The Holy Sacrifice commenced immediately. At the elevation she prostrated herself in adoration, and at the communion she walked to the altar, and, after receiving her Lord in the most Blessed Sacrament, knelt for half an hour in thanksgiving. The excitement of the people was at its height; all returned thanks to God. The Sisters in particular were overwhelmed with joy. Their well-beloved superior walked to the convent without assistance, and took her meal with the community. Her voice and strength returned at the same time.

This miracle made great noise abroad, and published the glory of St. Anthelme. On recovering her health under these extraordinary circumstances, she felt in her soul an increase of zeal for the glory of God and compassion for the miseries of her neighbor. Her reputation for sanctity was such that a great number of sick relied on her prayers to obtain their health, and their confidence was rewarded with recovery. Among these we find a person belonging to the most honorable family of Torez—Fanny de Vaux. She was always troubled with weak sight, but at seventeen years of age the malady was aggravated so as to render work impossible. In 1826 she was sent to Belley to spend some time with one of her uncles, under-prefect of the city, and there she had recourse to Mother St. Joseph, who obtained her cure. She herself relates the circumstance in a letter written on the following day to her father.

"My eyes," she said, "were so tired that I could not spend a day without a bandage of several doubles over my eyes, and over that a green shade to shut out the light. I could not stay any place but in a darkened room; and if the door were opened or a light allowed in, I could not restrain my tears, the pain being so excessive, and for an hour after I suffered from this. Greatly afflicted at my condition, my aunt and cousins told me to place all my hopes in God, and they spoke to me of the superior of the Sisters of St. Joseph in Belley, whose reputation for sanctity had already been confirmed by many miracles. I applied no more remedies. They asked her to come to see me. For a long time her humility deterred her. At last, at their continued solicitations, she was induced to come. She told me to have confidence, and to commence a novena in honor of the Blessed Virgin, and promise her to wear a blue woollen dress for one year. Last Sunday, the seventh day of the novena, she came to see me and to reanimate my sinking faith. After some moments she arose as if to leave. I caught hold of her to detain her, and she stood still. 'Poor child!' she said, 'let me see your eyes.' I raised my veil. 'Take off this veil and band,' she added; 'you will need them no more.' She remained immovable again. I thought she prayed. After that she touched my eyes and led me to the window. I was astonished at finding myself able to look into the garden without being tired. She sent for a lighted candle; the light did not fatigue my eyes. Then she knelt and made a fervent prayer, in which all present joined. She arose from her knees and sent me for an 'Imitation of Christ.' I read four pages by the candle-light. From that time I read and worked by day and candle-light. I feel neither cold nor the sun. Yesterday, the last day of the novena, all that remained to be done was to assist at the Holy Sacrifice of the Mass. The 'Te Deum' was chanted and a Mass of thanksgiving offered." *

Some time after, a young servant whom Mother St. Joseph had placed with a physician took consumption. The doctor, convinced that she would soon die, asked Mother St. Joseph to take her again, and sent her, not without much trouble, to the community. On her arrival, on Friday in Passion week, the young patient conjured Mother St. Joseph to obtain her restoration to health. This she promised to do on Holy Thursday, and immediately commenced a novena of prayers. During this novena the malady only increased; but it was remarked that the hemorrhages and the cough stopped when Mother St. Joseph put her hand under the head of the patient to raise her up. The doctor tried to find a cause for this, and himself raised her in exactly the same manner, but without effecting similar results. Charity constantly kept the Mother near her pro-

* See Appendix.

tégée, until one day the priest, noticing her fatigue, said: "Since God allows you to relieve this patient, perhaps you could communicate the same virtue to what you wear. You ought to assure yourself of this." On the next day she could have said: "I have practised obedience, and my cord has worked as my hands." After that, the Sisters, in the absence of their superior, had only to place her cord on the head of the sick girl to arrest the cough and hemorrhage. Nevertheless, her strength diminished every day. On the eve of Holy Thursday the Sisters believed she was dying, and sent for the priest, who administered extreme unction. Mother St. Joseph alone was fully confident of her recovery. On Thursday morning she had her clothing brought to the bed and assured her that in seven hours she would get up, dress, and hear a Mass of thanksgiving, for which a priest was to come. At the specified hour the girl exclaimed: "My God! I am cured. You have accomplished your work." She got up, went to the chapel to hear Mass, sang the canticles, and on the same day made the Stations of the Cross.

She had great devotion to St. Anthelme, and obtained, besides her own cure, many other favors. One day her niece, a child of three or four years of age, was on the point of dying; the doctor begged her to go away, so as not to witness the painful sight. But she wrapped the child in a shawl, took it to the tomb of St. Anthelme, and prayed there. In a few moments the child opened its eyes and recognized her. The Sisters who had followed her were all surprised, and said: "Mother, she moves well."

She replied: "What is there astonishing in seeing a child move?"

She took back her niece perfectly restored.

Another time a child of eleven or twelve years, deaf and dumb from its birth, was brought to her, being a sister to one of the religious, who asked her to obtain speech and hearing for it. She promised all her prayers, and had the community join in a novena. Some days after, a lady, seeing the child, pitied her on account of her hopeless condition. Mother St. Joseph said: "Yes, the child is to be pitied just now; but on the Feast of St. Anthelme she will be cured."

"If persons heard you," said the lady, "they would believe you deranged.

"Why," said the superior, "all the community are praying; and is not God kind and powerful enough to cure the child? It is more extraordinary that you should doubt His goodness."

The day of the feast arrived; she prayed with fervor during Mass to Him who cured the deaf and dumb man spoken of in the Gospel, and begged a renewal of the miracle in favor of this little child. "Your power, Lord, and your goodness, are now what they were then." At the consecration the sound of the bell so terrified the child that she was about to run away, and, on the Sister's speaking to her, she manifested still greater fear. She was cured.

CHAPTER XX.

FOUNDATION OF A HOUSE OF PROVIDENCE FOR THE AGED AND ORPHANS—HER CHARITY TOWARDS THEM.

TO be faithful to the spirit of their institute, the Sisters of St. Joseph should labor for their own perfection and sanctification, and the good of their neighbor in all their spiritual and temporal necessities. Mother St. Joseph never lost sight of this twofold end, and, while applying herself to the first, was careful not to forget the second.

Endowed with a just and a naturally orderly mind, she sought on her arrival at Belley to supply all the wants of the poor and to diminish the general causes of misery. Not content with establishing the distribution of alms, she invented means of labor for the population; and the day she purchased the chapter-house she projected the foundation of a home for the aged and for orphans. After her extraordinary recovery on St. Anthelme's day, she experienced great remorse for not having fulfilled her charitable design, and, without delay, she opened the refuge, to which she gave the name of Providence. She commenced by taking three poor children whose young mother had recently died. Shortly afterwards she received a little boy five years of age, who was paralyzed and dumb from weakness and bad treatment. No one believed that he could live, but the charitable religious kept him fifteen days in her own room, and gave him all possible care; even bathed him in warm wine to strengthen his limbs and heal the bruises inflicted on him. At the end of that time he was able to walk and speak. She then paid his board in a good family; later on she had him taught a trade, and she ever watched over him with a mother's solicitude.

In one of her visits to the poor she met with a family of laborers in which several of the members were sick. They were in want of everything, and would not resort to begging. Among the others, crouched in a corner, was an old man, almost stupid from want of nourishment. She gave them all the means she had with her, and on returning to the community she immediately sent the clothing and provision she deemed necessary. After some days, so as to lessen expenses, she delicately managed to ask these high-souled people to give her the care of the old man as a boarder in her new foundation. The request was reluctantly complied with, and he was the first to enter the collection of old persons called the Boarders of Providence, in allusion to the only support and the name of the new institute. She was soon happy in counting twenty-five orphans and twelve old persons. She studied their tastes, their habits, and even the caprices of the latter, so as not to contradict them. Her principal recreation was to go among them, and bestow touching marks of her devotedness. They, on their part, repaid her with gratitude. In her absence they were sad, and ill-humor made them complain; but when she appeared, their faces beamed with joy. They listened attentively to her advice, always given with pleasing amiability. She left to no one the care of preparing them for the reception of the last sacraments. When she saw death approach, she redoubled her efforts to sweetly direct towards heaven all their thoughts and hopes. The orphans were an object of her maternal and tender care, joined with a great firmness in bending their will to love obedience, industry, and the observance of exact discipline.

The establishment did not in any way interfere with those founded before it. The visits to the poor and the prisons, and the distribution of alms, were continued as before, but the wants of the institution exceeded its resources. By her inventive genius she readily supplied these.

The first means was labor. The religious, the very young children, and the aged, all labored according to the measure of their strength and capacity. Besides the raising of silk-worms, which occupied them several months of the year, and various kinds of needlework, she established in the house a place for preparing church articles and vestments. While teaching these works she sought to instil into all a spirit of order and economy in affairs.

The donations of M. Guillomot and of other charitably-disposed persons aided in the commencement; but as the number of inmates was ever on the increase, the supplies became insufficient, and the house was in danger of proving a failure, if God had not provided a second founder in the worthy benefactor M. Goux.

Louis Francis Goux, a doctor, possessed of a considerable fortune, entered as boarder, in 1825, at the hospice at Belley. Remaining nearly always in his own room, and not speaking to any one in the house, he lived in absolute isolation from the world. Although a stranger to the impressions of faith, a sympathetic feeling towards mankind led him to relieve the poor; and, as his manner of life did not permit him to do it himself, he made donations through some charitable person. Having heard of the life and labors of Mother St. Joseph, he wished to become acquainted with her.

Though he had a mind not easily to be impressed, it did not take him long to judge that she was worthy of absolute confidence. Certain that the donations he gave could not be disposed of more advantageously than she would use them, he gave them to her personally and unconditionally. The first relations of M. de Goux and Mother St. Joseph date 1827. He soon complained that she did not give him a large enough share in her good works, and he wished, by giving her frequent sums, to provide for the future wants of the aged and the orphan. His hostile sentiments against religion gradually yielded, owing to the influence of the virtues of Mother St. Joseph; but he always retained a prejudice against the good Bishop of Belley. Mother St. Joseph, who revered the bishop, left nothing undone to dispel this feeling. His grace desired a piece of land still known as the Bishop's Enclosure, which belonged to M. Goux. She was charged to obtain it, and succeeded only after the greatest persistence. There existed in the mind of M. Goux a dread that part of what he gave was remitted to the bishop. He constantly repeated to Mother St. Joseph that it was to herself that he made these gifts; that he intended she should always retain her ownership and administration, even if she returned to the world. His grace, to whom these conditions were submitted, did not foresee any inconvenience, and permitted their acceptance. We will see later the pain and distress of which they were the occasion.

In 1829 M. Goux, feeling his strength diminish, wished to give all his wealth to Mother St. Joseph; but, having met with invincible resistance, he decided, September 29, 1829, to make a will, making his nephew, M. M——, universal legatee.

In April, 1830, the charitable old man lost his sight, and this misfortune increased his habitual sadness. His only relief was found in the conversation and the care of Mother St. Joseph, which she continued until his death, in November, 1831. She had the consolation to see him die in the most Christian sentiments. M. M——, inheritor of the wealth of M. Goux, contrary to his expectations, experienced a lively gratitude towards Mother St. Joseph, and testified this not alone by words and letters, but also by munificent gifts. But, alas! for the instability of human gratitude. Soon after, in the midst of the political passions that agitated the city, he changed his conduct, and, pretending that the Mother had received only on deposit the amount given by M. Goux, he made an assignment in January, 1833, before the tribunal of Belley, by which she would be required to return him 59,000 francs. The case was pleaded during four sessions before a numerous audience. The tribunal, in the absence of the chief ordinary, was presided over by a judge whose opinions were against lay congregations. These sentiments were known to all the city; but the disinterestedness and charity of Mother St. Joseph had placed her above popular prejudice, and every one feared an unfavorable result, not for the religious, but for the continuance of the work she had established. Accordingly, many welcomed with enthusiasm a judgment giving her the advantage of longer time to justify her cause on all points. The day of trial came. Mother St. Joseph went to visit the poor, without being troubled concerning the suit. She replied to an observation made by some one: "Why should I be uneasy when the good God has charged St. Michael to gain my cause?" Her advocate defended with rare eloquence, and when he finished, had gained the suit. All assembled said: "This is not a man that spoke; it is an angel."

About this time the old chapel was found too small, and it was deemed necessary to build a new one. While examining the work one day, she noticed a mason named Columbat taking up on a ladder a large stone which he wished to set in the wall. On perceiving him she repeated the prayer she said each morning in honor of the Blessed Virgin to protect the workmen. At the same instant a terrific cry was heard. The unfortunate man had fallen from the ladder. "Blessed Virgin, save him!" cried she, looking towards where he had fallen. The man was standing, and, when she asked if he were hurt, he answered in the negative; and he again ascended the ladder. She blessed God, and fervently thanked her whom she had never invoked in vain.

When the work was completed, she wanted two hundred francs to finish the required payment. She was sick in bed, when she thought of going to Vespers, during which a procession of the Blessed Sacrament was to take place. When our Lord was near in sacramental presence, she said: "Master, you know all things; consequently, why I have come here. I want money to pay the men who worked on your house; you know this—give me sufficient." After benediction, despite the urgent request of her companion to the contrary, she took a circuitous path home. She had not gone far when she met an old man, who said to her: "Mother, I am glad to meet you. You engaged my mind all the time of the procession. The thought to give you two hundred francs constantly distracted me, and it was only after I had promised to give the sum that I could at all pray." The Mother thanked him, and admired the touching goodness of her divine Master in her regard.

CHAPTER XXI.

SHE FULFILS THE DUTIES OF ASSISTANT.

THE charge of assistant which Mother St. Joseph had received did not allow her to concentrate her labors on affairs at Belley. She was obliged to take an active part in the general administration of the congregation. She went to Bourg several times during the year to attend the meeting of the council. She assisted also at the general retreats, profiting by the confidence that the religious placed in her to cement the union of their hearts; and she always gave an example of affectionate submission and great respect towards the venerable Mother St. Benedict. Her intimate and frequent relations with Bishop Devie allowed her to be of great use to the congregation. As assistant, she was also charged to visit a specified number of the houses, and she annually acquitted herself of this duty with great care. During these visitations she took pleasure in drawing out the qualities of each Sister, and assisted them greatly by her advice in the correction of their faults. She knew also how to prevent the reception of subjects who might become an obstacle to the good of the community; but before sending them away, she ordinarily asked that they be confided to her, and she applied herself with fervor to render them worthy of their vocation by her example and the firmness of her direction. Many owed their perseverance in the religious life to her. The death of Sisters always gave her great sorrow. Her spiritual daughters knew this, and the knowledge gave rise to a touching precaution taken by a lay Sister named St. Bridget. This good religious had predicted her death a month previous. In the interval she begged Mother de la Croix to send her superior on a visitation of the houses. "Our Mother must not see me die," she said. "I wish her spared the grief. I must be buried and the infirmary be in order before she returns." Her demands were so urgent that the superior acquiesced, and all happened as she desired. Mother St. Joseph experienced great pain on the death of Sister St. Lucy, a religious of great piety and perfect regularity, and possessed of an open character, always obliging towards her companions, who loved and venerated her as a saint. They saw but one fault in her, which was that, in the fulfilment of her office as portress, she would not immediately attend the bell-call when she was at prayer in the chapel. The priest, after administering Extreme Unction, believing her hearing impaired by approaching death, could not refrain from praising her virtue. He exhorted the Sisters to follow her example, so as to end their lives by a holy death. Mother St. Joseph at first dared not interrupt him, but at last, knowing that the dying Sister heard his praises, she could no longer remain silent, and said: "Father, you are mistaken; you have not known and observed Sister Lucy so closely as I have. She was often negligent in the discharge of her duties, her sweetness arose from an extreme indifference, and her amiability was purely natural; therefore I beg you to unite your prayers with ours to obtain the pardon of her infidelities." Some time after she went to the bedside and spoke to the dying Sister of the loving mercy of the Blessed Virgin. While listening to her the Sister seemed to suffer less agony, and spoke of Mary with an incomparable tenderness and confidence. She thanked the superior for giving so true a picture of her, adding: "When father praised me, I was tormented with pride and vain-glory; but your words brought back to my soul truth and peace." Afterwards Mother St. Joseph gave this example to teach her Sisters never to praise the dying.

The works of charity which she established at Belley would have exhausted the strength of a soul less active and less generous than her own; but she always held herself prepared to relieve the unfortunate whom Providence placed in her way. One evening she felt a strong impulse forcing her to go to see a family of whose condition she was ignorant. Arriving at the door, she heard a conversation, interrupted by loud sobs. A young girl said to her mother: "Let us not throw ourselves in the well—it will be a disgrace; we can go to the bank of the Rhone, keep close to one another, and the current will carry us beyond recovery."

"My child," said the mother, "it is a crime to destroy one's self."

"Yes, but the alternative given me is also a crime; death before dishonor."

Mother St. Joseph knocked at the door, entered, seated herself, and asked for a glass of water. After a few moments, she related with tears in her eyes their own history, and added: "These two persons are in the city; they know not the infinite goodness of God nor the power of charity. Like many others, they too call me the 'good Mother,' and it seems that I have a right to their confidence and to a share in their sorrows." At these words the two women threw themselves at her feet, and asked pardon of God for the crime they had contemplated. They told her that a miser who had robbed them of their estate wished the young girl to sell her virtue to him; and, on being repelled, he purposed to sell on the following day all that belonged to them. Mother St. Joseph sought him out and forewarned him of approaching death, and threatened him with publishing everywhere his base designs. She offered him an adequate sum to pay the debt. After repeated refusals, the man was finally overcome, and he gave her the quit-claim deed, which she hastened to take to her protégées. She afterwards set them up in business in Lyons, and herself instructed them in the arts of commerce. She frequently examined their books, corrected their inventory, and taught them to keep an exact account of their affairs. The good God blessed them. The mother was surrounded with every comfort and care until her death, and the daughter still enjoys an independent livelihood.

In passing a hotel one day, Mother St. Joseph was asked to enter and speak to a stranger who was apparently deranged and in despair. She complied, and was standing a long time near him before she attracted his attention. She was at a loss to know how to open a conversation with him. At last, after having interiorly prayed to God, she took the man by the arm and said: "Good-day, my friend; I am happy to see you. You don't recognize me, I perceive?"

These words interrupted the course of his thoughts, and he replied in some unintelligible words.

"But you ask no information concerning your family," she said.

"Oh! if you can give me any, I will be most grateful."

"Yes, my friend; all your people are in good health, but exceedingly anxious and distressed on account of not hearing from you. Tell me, then, why you don't write to them."

He believed her initiated into the secrets of his family, and he unhesitatingly told all his troubles to her. He was a wealthy miller, who, by his too great readiness to supply all who called on him, had brought his wife and eight children to absolute want and misery; his mill was sold and himself about to be arrested for indebtedness. She wept at the recital, and planned means to relieve his distress.

When he had finished, she said: "Is it thus, my friend, that you outrage Providence, ever kind and beneficent? I take charge of all. To-morrow I will return to see you."

' But the warrant for my arrest is issued. If I am known, I shall be thrown into prison."

"No, no, it will be nothing. I will take charge of you and your debts, and will restore you to your family."

A ray of hope entered the heart of the unhappy man, who followed with his eyes, until she disappeared, the angel whom God had sent to him.

On the morrow she returned and gave him some money to defray his present expenses; but as the sum required to save the honor and restore the lost wealth of this man was too great to be obtained in a small city, the Mother went to Lyons. She first asked the assistance of Our Lady of Fourvières, and then called on several houses in the city, where she received generous donations. Among others, a rich banker, well known to her by reputation, gave her several handfuls of silver, and, being himself astonished at his large offering, she said to him: "It is not you who gives; it is Mary who gives through your hands."

The men in many places not only gave

for themselves, but also introduced her to their friends and obtained additional aid from them. In two days she realized more than fifty thousand francs. Having then obtained permission to settle the affairs of the poor miller, she assembled his creditors, paid his obligations, purchased the mill, and returned to the exiled father to tell him of his freedom to return, and live happy and honorably. It is impossible to picture the joy and tender gratitude of this man or the humble simplicity of the Mother, who looked upon what she had accomplished as only a natural consequence of human sympathy.

When the village of Vivien, near Belley, was entirely destroyed by fire, Mother St. Joseph went to the scene of devastation, and returned some hours after with two carriages having twenty-two little girls in them. These she placed in care of the Sisters, and herself went to the city in quest of provisions for the sufferers, which she conveyed to them and distributed with her own hands.

The prisoners were always an object of special interest to her. She mended their clothing and showed most tender solicitude for them. They, in return, confided to her all their troubles and gave her messages for their families. Often she obtained for the poorest among them permission to go to their homes in harvest-time, on condition that they returned to fill out their terms of imprisonment. They never failed to return, as the good Mother, they said, was their security before the magistrates, who, knowing the charity of Mother St. Joseph, could refuse her nothing. She never went to the prisons without a supply of provisions, which she distributed according to the wants of each and with a desire to please all. She devoted hours to the instruction of those ignorant of the truths of faith. She often said of them: "They are not so guilty as supposed; they would not have committed these faults had they known of the existence of God and the immortality of their souls. They let themselves be carried away by their evil passions, because they were not instructed in their religion and knew nothing of God; and what human strength could repress or restrain them?"

CHAPTER XXII.

HER ZEAL IN FAVORING VOCATIONS TO THE PRIESTHOOD.

HER charity was extended to all mankind; but her fervent love for the Church inspired her with a great zeal to aid in the education of young men destined to the priesthood. While still in the world, she devoted part of the proceeds of her labor to assist poor seminarians. During her stay at Chazay she encouraged and aided the studies of three young men, who afterwards became priests; and she interested in this work several rich persons of the city. At Belley, when she met in poor Christian families children with good dispositions and inclined to the priesthood, she would not rest until she obtained of Bishop Devie their gratuitous admission into some seminary. If the wants of the diocese did not allow the prelate to accede to her desires, she had her community perform works of supererogation to accomplish her end. The proceeds of the silk-worms were particularly devoted to this. She bought books for the less fortunate, washed their clothing, and watched over them as a tender mother. When necessary, she solicited aid from the wealthy, and even borrowed money for this purpose; and she never permitted any ecclesiastical vocation to be blighted for want of resources wherewith to pursue the usual course of studies, when the subjects gave promise of becoming priests.

One day a poor shepherd, about seventeen or eighteen years of age, came to her and said, with unaffected simplicity: "Mother, I want to be a priest."

"Well, my friend, who told you to be a priest?"

"No one."

"How did you think of it?"

"I don't know; it always comes to my mind."

"Have you spoken to your pastor?"

"No; I came to tell you."

"Do you know how to read?"

"No."

"How do you occupy your time while guarding your sheep?"

"I think of the good God, and say to myself that I want to be a priest."

"And why do you want to be a priest?"

"To go to convert those far away who need conversion."

The good Mother asked him no further. She gave him a book, and told him to return the following Sunday, if he could read. The young shepherd returned on the appointed day, knowing how to read after his own style, though not correctly. The Mother wrote to a parish priest, recommending the young man to his attention, and begging him to give him some lessons. His progress was so rapid that in less than six months he was advanced enough to enter a seminary. He became a priest, and died a missionary in China.

Another time a young libertine came to the convent to see a religious. Mother St. Joseph, having a supernatural knowledge in his regard, went herself to the parlor. She strongly, forcibly reproached him with the scandalous disorders of his life, adding: "Unhappy man! you have merited eternal misery; nevertheless, God looks upon you with eyes of mercy. You will be converted, will become a priest, and tremble as often as your hand is raised to absolve others."

The young man sneered at her prediction, and ran through the town repeating: "Mother St. Joseph is assured that I am to become a monk."

After a few years he entered a seminary, and became fervent and mortified. Appointed pastor in a parish near Belley, he edified all by the practice of the most admirable charity. He distributed all he possessed to the poor, and, though his mother had frequently renewed his wardrobe, he was often in want of clothing. One day in the month of January, on returning from administering the last sacraments to a dying person, he met a poor old man barefooted in the snow and shivering with cold. Moved by compassion at the sight, he took off his own shoes and stockings, gave them to the beggar, and returned to his residence. This was his last charitable deed. He was attacked with pneumonia, and after having the consolation of a visit from Mother St. Joseph, whom he styled his spiritual mother, he died a holy death.

The life of this worthy servant of God continued to be marked by prodigies, and persons came to her for relief in the miseries of the soul, as well as those of the body. A young priest in one of the colleges in the country came to open his conscience to her. For some years he had devoted himself to the study of the profane sciences, rather than to the exercise of prayer and the fulfilment of his sacerdotal functions, and he now felt his faith shaken. Some of the mysteries—above all, that of the Trinity—he believed incompatible with reason. The good Mother did her best to show that the word mystery in itself indicated that reason could not grasp its signification, that a creature so weak as man should not hope to fathom the impenetrable secrets of God, and that nature at each step showed mysteries as incomprehensible as those of religion; but this reasoning, so palpable to a soul in the right path, made no impression whatever on him.

She felt deeply touched at the misery of this soul. She offered a long and fervent prayer to God. The young professor remained quiet, not daring to interrupt her. At last she seemed to him to recover from an ecstasy, and said to him: "Look and believe!"

In an instant there was shed from the centre of the ceiling a light that illumined the whole apartment. Its point diverged into a triangle, which rested on the head of the professor. He thought the light was but a passing reflection of the sun, but, on having closed the window-blinds, it became more luminous. He knelt down and confessed with a lively faith one God in Three Persons, and ever after applied himself to fulfil with exactitude all the duties of his calling. He himself several times related this to the present Superior of Bordeaux.

God frequently consoled her by the appearance in her room of an extraordinary light. She told this to a young priest with whose family she was acquainted, and in whom she felt great interest. He was little disposed to believe this prodigy, when one day, while visiting the Mother, the walls and ceiling of her room were entirely covered with luminous and regularly-arranged rays of great brilliancy, which remained a long time, and gradually disappeared. The sun was not shining at the time, and nothing natural could explain the phenomenon. Shortly after, the same priest, while preaching in one of the churches of Paris, was surprised to see Mother St. Joseph directly in front of the pulpit among the audience. His servant, who assisted at the sermon, also saw her. As soon as he descended from the pulpit, he sent a messenger to tell her he wished to see her in the sacristy; but she had disappeared. He wrote immediately to Belley, where he was told that she had not been absent from her community. The Mother herself wrote to him some time after, and, without entering into any explanation, she made useful and pointed remarks on the style of his discourse and the intentions that should direct him in announcing the word of God. This priest is still exercising the holy ministry, and he related these two facts in 1864, and showed the letters of Mother St. Joseph, which he carefully treasures.

A circumstance analogous to this occurred in 1835, in the case of a young person whom she had rescued from danger and placed in a virtuous family. She frequently gave her advice, either through letters or by means of trustworthy persons, and she never for a moment forgot the child. One day Mother St. Joseph was overwhelmed by unaccountable sadness, and, according to her custom, she had recourse to prayer, wherein our Lord made known to her that this young person underwent severe combats. "Lord," she said, "you know the evil; give me the remedy. Let my good angel visit this child." The same day, however, as she never omitted to employ natural means, she wrote to her nephew, Father Montceni, then at Lyons, to visit this young person and advise her. He went at once to fulfil the wish of his aunt, and was not a little astonished on being told by the young girl that she had received a visit from Mother St. Joseph the day before, and she wished him to thank her for her kindness. He was at a loss for an answer, knowing that his aunt had not left Belley. However, to assure himself of the truth, he went to Belley, and there learned that she had not left the city. When he manifested surprise, she said: "I sent my angel guardian to give the message for me." Father Montceni, present almoner of the community at Bordeaux, related this fact himself.

In the midst of her various labors she did not forget her vow to go to the Indies if her superiors allowed her, and she occasionally asked the fulfilment. She had prepared herself for indescribable sufferings on leaving her Sisters and her works at Belley; above all the poor, who found in her a true Mother, and she reciprocated their feelings. Her request to go to the Indies was always refused, but a separation from all she held dear was nevertheless to take place. In 1837 M. de la Croix, Vicar-General of Belley and superior of the Sisters of St. Joseph, was nominated Bishop of Gap. This holy priest obtained from Bishop Devie leave for Mother St. Joseph to go into the new diocese to found a novitiate and other houses of the congregation. The granting of the request demanded a great sacrifice on the part of Mgr. Devie; nevertheless, it was granted on condition that she should remain five years in the Diocese of Gap, and then return to Belley.

CHAPTER XXIII.

PROGRESS OF MOTHER ST. JOSEPH IN THE SPIRITUAL LIFE.

BEFORE accompanying Mother St. Joseph to the new scene of her labors in Gap, it is well to take a general view of her progress in the spiritual life, and the particular circumstances which favored this progress.

From her infancy she had been the recipient of most signal graces. These graces continued throughout her youth, and seemed shaped, as it were, with one end—to have constantly before her the service of God and of her neighbor. Father Tauvette, her director until her entrance into religion, was a man of great piety, an open heart, and possessing an amiable simplicity.

He admired the ways by which the Holy Spirit conducted his penitent; he saw the glory of God in the manifestation of the extraordinary gifts she received; and he feared not to mention these in her presence on the day of her reception into religion. Jane herself, whose nature was as open as it was generous, spoke freely of the extraordinary graces she had received; for it seemed to her that all the world ought to thank God with her. This disposition met with no opposition before her entrance into religion, and continued in the community of St. Peter (the old) and at Chazay, where her superiors and companions knew all that God wrought in her and through her. It was like a second nature, formed by a habit of twenty years, of which she never completely divested herself.

On arriving at Belley, in 1819, she had for ordinary confessor M. Guillomot, who showed the greatest confidence in her, and who found nothing to blame in the habits of her life. But God, who had His own design, ordained that she should meet in M. Pichat, superior of a small seminary, a director better suited to the wants of her soul. He perceived at once the great danger in which her humility was of being lost, and with it all the other virtues in her soul. He forbade her to speak of the extraordinary graces God had accorded her, and forced her to moderate her too fiery nature; and he was unsparing in the humiliations he imposed on her with the purpose to counteract the manifest veneration she received from others. One day he told her to come at a specified hour and, in presence of the persons with whom he might be engaged, ask him to hear her general confession. Next day, at the hour agreed upon, she came, and found M. Pichat accompanied by all the professors, and he in the act of stepping into a carriage. For a moment she was undecided what to do; then, suppressing her feelings, she approached and said: "Father, I wish you to hear my general confession, if you please."

M. Pichat listened seriously; then, turning towards the professors, remarked:

"Persons have well said that Mother St. Joseph has a light and extravagant mind, and this act of hers convinces me of its truth. Judge for yourselves if the time she selects to ask me to hear her general confession is well chosen."

She withdrew in confusion, but happy in having performed an act of obedience and drawn on herself a great humiliation.

His direction placed her under a restraint which was before unknown to her. It seemed that she had lost that holy liberty and generosity which she had previously experienced. She told him that she believed he was laboring under a delusion concerning her, and that his direction was not suitable for her. He obliged her to yield this opinion, and wrote her a long letter, in which he showed her that the way of obedience is always the sure and safe way, even should the director be mistaken; and he then pointed out the snares laid for her by the demon, adding: "Since the will of God has placed you under my direction you have experienced many trials, but these were necessary to purify you from a great number of imperfections which you would not have perceived, and with which you never reproached yourself. You would always have retained these if God had not subjected you to trials. The habit you had of speaking too frequently of yourself, and which you must relinquish, both in conversation and in letters; and the hasty and often harsh replies you make to others—in fine, your great sensibility to supposed wrongs done you, and unworthy motives in others—all go to prove that you are far from having acquired the virtues of Jesus Christ, who himself says: 'Learn of me, for I am meek and humble of heart'; and, again: 'Father, forgive them, for they know not what they do.'"

The severity of Father Pichat soon gave place to goodness, which was the chief element in his nature.

One day, knowing that Mother St. Joseph was a prey to sadness, he wrote to her:

"An inspiration to write you a few words of consolation is given me, my dear Sister, and I will not suppress it; for it seems to me you are in distress. When the Celestial Spouse of your soul hides Himself, and appears to be angry, it would then seem that the trials sent by Almighty

God are indeed hard. But make a generous effort; let us bow respectfully to these holy chastisements, and, with a little patience, we will not be long in finding a hidden source of strength and sweetness. I recommend you, then, to hold to your firm confidence in God, in order that, as in temporal affairs you have often learned that when all seemed lost it was then that Providence was nearest and most attentive to your wants, so in the spiritual life you should be convinced, without even the shadow of a doubt, that the more you perceive the weakness, misery, and malice of your own soul, the nearer you are to feel the power of the grace and goodness of God, which will teach you to divest yourself of self-love, and awaken in you a life of faith. In the spiritual warfare, as in a battle, the enemy often wounds us, and it is necessary to keep up our courage; for in the war of the Spirit against the flesh, he is considered victorious who ceases not to fight, and strife must be carried on until the last sigh. Patience, confidence, obedience, and abandonment—four words I wish you to keep in your heart as a bouquet of myrrh. Myrrh is bitter, but it is its bitterness that preserves what it touches. Adieu! Let us shelter ourselves in the Sacred Heart. You know with what affection I desire your peace, in God alone. PICHAT."

Mother St. Joseph, having recognized the wisdom and the great virtues of M. Pichat, placed the most absolute confidence in him. He fulfilled the duty of extraordinary confessor of the community until his death, in 1827, and it was to him that Mother St. Joseph had recourse to recover calm and peace when the trials imposed on her by Bishop Devie seemed above her strength.

Some years after his arrival at Belley, he considered it best to reserve the direction of Mother St. Joseph to himself. The greatest severities of Father Pichat were sweetnesses compared with the trials to which Bishop Devie's direction subjected her. It was at the time when the prodigies attributed to her gained the greatest publicity that his care of her soul commenced. A man of faith and an eminent theologian, he was on his guard about rejecting these facts because they had supernatural appearances; but he feared, and with reason, the illusion of self-love and the danger of pride. He exacted from his penitent an exact and detailed account of the lights and the supernatural gifts she received. If the least contradiction was apparent in her declaration, or between the prediction and the accomplishment of events, he pointed it out. He framed a rule of conduct for her, and he allowed her to leave his presence only after receiving some great humiliation. If he did not give it in speaking to her, a letter supplied the omission. He was himself accustomed to most austere practices of mortification, and he considered them of great efficacy for the advancement of souls in virtue. Consequently, during many years he obliged Mother St. Joseph to take the discipline three times a day, without mentioning the numerous other instruments of penance. She said: "I might call my director an executioner."

Exterior mortification was nothing in

comparison with that of the will and the imagination. Every act of the day was submitted to the minutest rule. Oral prayers, subjects for meditation, reading, the time passed before the Blessed Sacrament, the practices of piety and mortification, permission to absent herself when the service of her neighbor required—all was determined by the director, and she obeyed punctually in the smallest matters.

Knowing her ability in the management of business, he constantly gave her the missions requiring most labor at Belley and in other parts of the diocese, and he allowed her to undertake works of charity which necessitated her absence. Nevertheless, the necessity did not prevent him chiding her too frequent journeys, as also her too frequent intercourse with seculars. When she gave an account of the different missions, he would not listen to anything referring to herself, but would interrupt her, saying: "See, my child, how you love to speak of yourself and make known all you do. You are full of self-love."

Her room was at all times open to the Sisters. One of them slept in her room;

consequently, it was impossible to conceal all her practices of mortification. The Sisters, moved with compassion at seeing a person already worn with fatigue and long sickness subject herself to rigorous austerities, went to the bishop, complained of her manner of life, and asked him to interpose his authority. He satisfied their minds, but sent immediately for the Superior, and said to her: "You are in every act animated by pride; you have either spoken of your austerities or practised them in public, so as to proclaim that you are treading a higher way than others." She listened on her knees to these reproaches, and when he had finished she asked a penance. He obliged her to take the discipline an additional time that day during the recitation of the psalm "Miserere." One of the Sisters who generally accompanied her was often a witness of these harsh reprimands. Under this excessive severity Bishop Devie concealed a great affection. He recognized in her a privileged soul, whom he wished to aid in the rapid and sure progress towards perfection. He obliged her to receive Holy Communion every day, without making any account of the disquietude of conscience, which, after all, was occasioned by the reproaches of her director. In 1836, during a protracted illness which prevented her from fasting, he gave orders that the Holy Communion be taken to her at midnight, and many times he himself performed this act of charity.

When we now consider, after so great an interval, the result of these trials, it seems easy to trace, in part at least, the ways of divine Providence. In the early portion of her life Mother St. Joseph had literally followed the inspirations of the Holy Spirit, mingled with the impulses of an ardent, generous, and energetic soul. One would suppose that God would allow this expansive nature to open sweetly the treasures of goodness with which he had endowed her; and without doubt this would have resulted had she remained in the world, where she could tread the way of Christian perfection alone, with only the loving inspirations of God to guide her actions. But being called to the direction of others, and to subject many souls to the empire of strict religious discipline, she had to accustom herself to obey at all times, and particularly when obedience was painful. It was necessary that the flights of charity and of fervent devotedness to her neighbor be taught to yield to the duties of common life and to the thousand exigencies of the rule; for in a religious community the interior life is preserved only by a great fidelity in little things. For a long time she attracted from many about her marks of sympathy; she received at every step praise and applause; but, as true virtue is acquired only after having been purified in the crucible of tribulation and humiliation, God would have her walk in this last way during many years, until her soul was sufficiently imbued to accomplish the principal work for which she was destined.

CHAPTER XXIV.

MOTHER ST. JOSEPH FOUNDS THE CONGREGATION AT GAP.

WHEN the time for the fulfilment of the agreement made between the Bishops of Belley and of Gap had come, Bishop Devie sent for Mother St. Joseph, and said to her: "My child, I am resolved this time to allow you to go a great distance to do the work of your good Master." The Mother, believing that he would give her permission to go to the Indies, could not contain her joy; but when she learned that she was not to leave France, her joy was suddenly changed into sadness. In spite of her efforts to hide the appearance of any unusual trouble, she lost her appetite and her sleep, and the Sisters knew that she labored under the oppressive weight of grief. When asked the cause, she assumed her usual amiability, and assured them that nothing gave her occasion for sorrow. Soon, however, they suspected the true reason—she was to leave with M. de la Croix for Gap. One Sister pretended that our Lord made the revelation to her in prayer, and the news was soon spread through the whole house. Some of the religious hastened to ascertain the truth from Bishop Devie, who became very much embarrassed, and he feared it would be impossible for her to leave if the news were given in advance. He sent for her immediately, and reproached her for having made his project known. Accustomed to being falsely charged by her spiritual father, she did not at all seek to justify herself, and only asked for a penance, which was given her. She received orders to await the coming of a carriage to conduct her to Lyons, without allowing her any time for preparation or to see any person. After this act of severity on the part of her director, he took the part of a good and affectionate father. He gave her recommendations for the preservation of her health, and promised to continue their union by their prayers and by their letters. Besides the sum necessary for their travelling expenses, he gave her a number of gold pieces, with orders to use them for her personal wants only; and in case of sickness she was to return to Belley.

On the following day, December 18, when the people learned of the departure of Mother St. Joseph, there was a general outburst of sorrow, as well as murmurs against Bishop Devie. Messengers were immediately sent to Lyons to bring back at any price her who had sweetened the sorrows of the afflicted and consoled the miserable; but she was not to be found. No one had any idea of looking for her in the prison at Roane, where she had been sent by Bishop Devie. The messengers returned to Belley, convinced that she had gone to Gap.

She spent ten days with the Sisters in charge of the prison, and repressed her grief by the energy of her will and the practice of good works. Although subject to violent attacks of fever, she every day gave instructions to the prisoners, spent many hours at the foot of the altar, and animated the Sisters by her words and by her example in the perfect accomplishment of their sublime mission. She spoke with all the unction and fire that a generous heart experienced; and later the Sisters who had the happiness of seeing and hearing her at Roane said they could never forget the impression made by her conferences and discourses.

The two Sisters, St. Wilfrid and St. Mary, who intended to accompany her to Gap, rejoined her at the prison, taking with them the necessary clothing and effects; for in her hasty departure she had not taken anything with her. Mother St. Benoit, superior of the congregation at Bourg, went to visit her, and gave her true consolation. But she found greatest strength at the feet of Our Lady of Fourvières, towards whom she had ever preserved a most tender devotion. She frequently went to this chapel, the cradle of her religious life, and, placing her heart in that of Mary, offered her project of the new foundation, and begged the interior strength of which she felt herself in need.

On her arrival at Lyons she wrote a letter to the Sisters, and charged Sister St. Geneviève to ask Bishop Devie to give her in writing the advice he had given her on the day of her departure. Sister St. Geneviève, among other things, said in her reply: "I requested Bishop Devie to comply with your wish relative to the advice he gave you, and he seemed edified at your pious sentiments. He expressed a hope that the good God would bless you and reward your sacrifices, and that you may promote His glory in all you do for the good of souls. We hope this likewise, dear Mother, and our confidence sweetens the pain we feel for your absence; but this does not prevent our feeling your loss with all the intensity of which we are capable. We are in need of strength, as well as you are, from Him who aids all to carry their cross.

"I will send you in a few days the details of our dear community-life since you left, knowing you will always consider as your children those who will never cease to call you Mother. Remember that in this quality you are obliged to aid us by your fervent prayers, and do not believe you are dispensed from the fulfilment because you have adopted other children."

The bishop wrote to her on the 24th of December. His advice was condensed into five principal points: to apply herself in all things to attain to forgetfulness of self; never to speak of the extraordinary lights she had received or believed she had received; not to follow these without reflection, and only after being satisfied they were from God; to listen to the reasoning of others; and for one year not to give any advice to priests who might consult her. The letter shows the method of direction used by her director, and his great desire to separate the good grain of divine favor from the straw of the illusions of imagination that mingled itself with them.

"BELLEY, December 24, 1837.

"I believe, my dear daughter, I should tell you that the Bishop of Gap will spend the feast of Christmas at Marseilles. If you go to Lyons, as you propose, on Tuesday or Wednesday, you will not find him there. In any case, you had better wait a few days. I have informed him of your resting-place in Roane, and it is probable he will write to you. In case he does not, you had better leave in three days. Mother St. Benoit has given you a new proof of her goodness in going to see you at Lyons. I learned of her going from Sister Stanislaus, who visited me the day after you left. I saw her but a moment—long enough to know that she is doing all in her power to console the poor Sisters, who are deeply grieved at your departure. They are, however, all at their posts, and performing their duties with zeal and assiduity.

"You desire me to write a repetition of my advice, that you may understand it better. I recommend to you above all a great humility and forgetfulness of self. Often read the second chapter of the first book in à Kempis, and the seventh chapter of the third book. Avoid with special care speaking of the graces you have received, or believe you have received; for I am persuaded that there is a mixture in these, and that the straw and dust are confounded with the good grain. Besides, I place more value on one act of humility, resignation, penance, or charity towards our neighbor than on all possible inspirations. There certainly is more merit attached to one of these acts. Without advising you to dispel these interior lights, I wish you to follow them only after having consulted your superior by obedience, and

God in prayer and reflection. You need not tell how these inspirations come to you, but simply propose the means to the Sisters or others whom they concern. Listen to their reasons for and against, but above all do not neglect prayer. In regard to your particular advice to priests, it is agreed that for one year you will not give any, and that you will tell me what passes in your mind with regard to this prohibition. I repeat this in writing, and I have many proofs that you gave advice not at all suitable, though it was received with gratitude and followed with docility. On the whole, it seems to me you have too great confidence in yourself, and that you have not made use of the means Providence places at your disposal to discern whether these lights proceed from the devil, from self, or from God. The wisest course for you to pursue is to attach little importance to these movements, and always to delay their execution. Do all this without inquietude for the past, nor even for the present, when you act without reflection. In the latter case make a note, which you can communicate to me later. If you are humble, the remedy for all this will be very easy; for I believe that a love of distinction or desire of show in all things is existent in your imagination. Profit now by the opportunity to petition your Mother Mary for the light, courage, and humility necessary to you. I unite with you in prayer."

CHAPTER XXV.

HER ARRIVAL AT GAP—VISIT OF BISHOP DEVIE

THE Sisters of St. Joseph were established at Gap in 1671 by Bishop P. Marion, Bishop and Count of Gap, and up to the Revolution had several communities in the diocese. After an interval of nearly fifty years, Mother St. Joseph came with her two companions to unite the present and the past, and to re-establish her order in the place. They arrived at Gap on Saturday, December 29, 1837. Bishop de la Croix was detained at Corsica, on account of the inclemency of the season, and had not yet reached his episcopal city. He had written to Father Arnaud, vicar-general, to receive the Sisters of St. Joseph in the Convent of the Sacred Heart, of which he was superior; but the good old man was much embarrassed on their arrival, as it seemed impossible to him to have them lodge with the Ladies of the Sacred Heart, and he wanted to install them in the bishop's house, to punish, he said, the new bishop, who was proceeding too fast in business.

One of the largest houses in Gap had been procured for the work, for thirty-two thousand francs; but possession could not be had for two months. The garret only was vacant; but nothing had been prepared to receive the religious. Happily, the Community of the Sacred Heart, having been informed of the circumstances, were willing to lodge the three religious until the arrival of the bishop, who came on the 3d of January. The kind reception that was given her at this house lived always in the grateful memory of Mother St. Joseph. In after-life she often related the circumstances, and recalled the remembrance of the charity, piety, and great regularity of the Sisters of the Sacred Heart. On the day succeeding his arrival, the bishop went to see his old daughters from Belley, and on the 5th the Sisters were installed in the vacant part of the house destined for them. Mother St. Joseph's first care was to select the most appropriate place in the vacant rooms for chapel purposes. M. Pasquier, a wealthy and charitable jeweller in the city, sent her the necessary sacred vessels, and her friends at Lyons furnished ornaments and linens. She improvised a temporary altar, which she herself made of planks and ornamented as best she could. On the 12th the bishop said Mass in the chapel, and left the Most Blessed Sacrament there. The pious foundress derived the greatest consolation from this favor. Near her divine Master, she could want for nothing; and she said to Him, with child-like joy: "Lord, you ought to be content with us. You are poorly lodged, it is true; but still better than your spouses."

The opening of this foundation was attended with many difficulties. Bishop de la Croix had more undertakings than his means allowed him to complete; and, notwithstanding his willingness, it was impossible for him to aid the Sisters. They had no furniture. Mattresses, borrowed from the seminary and laid on the floor, served them for beds, and the trunks answered the purpose of chairs. In these trying circumstances she endeavored to maintain cheerfulness in the Sisters, but her efforts were not always successful. Sister St. Wilfrid, who was unaccustomed to these privations, felt their condition very sensibly, and, to relieve her mind and cheer her spirits, Mother St. Joseph would oblige her to get into a trunk, and then had her drawn around the room, telling her that few persons were so favored as to have a carriage drawn by religious. The Sister had to laugh at the apparent nonsense of the act, which satisfied the Mother.

One day, at dinner-time, she had said the "Benedicite," and waited for a Sister to ask the blessing; but the Sisters could not restrain their laughter, nor speak. One of them, being asked the cause of her inopportune laughter, said: "Mother, what will you bless? We have nothing on the table."

She opened the door of the chapel, and, turning towards the tabernacle, said:

"Lord, your spouses do not rely on you. Show them that confidence in your goodness is not in vain."

She returned, and, seating herself at the table, commenced the spiritual lecture. A few minutes afterwards some one knocked at the door, and, on opening, they found that a lady in the city had sent her servant with all the necessaries for a dinner. Mother St. Joseph went to thank this lady, who said: "I had my dinner prepared without thinking of you; but at the moment it should be served a thought came into my mind that the strange religious, my neighbors, were perhaps in want, and I sent the dinner to them."

Notwithstanding her efforts to console and strengthen her companions, the pious foundress was herself overwhelmed by great sadness. The severe direction of M. Devie resulted in disheartening this soul, so oppressed with sadness. Her custom of speaking freely to our Lord, and of communicating to others the lights and impressions she received, had been fought against incessantly, and discouragement and fear withheld her from undertaking any new work. During the first week of her arrival, a great number of postulants presented themselves, but she feared to receive them; and on the 16th of January, 1838, she wrote to Mgr. Devie: "Every time persons present themselves to us for reception my heart enlarges, and I repeat interiorly my refrain: 'It were better for me to have died last year than to live this year to prevent a great good, and perhaps accomplish a great evil.' I don't know why you cannot understand me. It is surely a punishment of my sins that has drawn all on me. I would not be troubled if the chastisement were only on myself. But, alas! for the new daughters of St. Joseph who are to come after me. This thought makes me tremble, and has made me defer until to-day the reception of six or seven only, to whom I have given my promise, and we must constantly receive them. I am tempted sometimes to say you are cruel. Will you, then, let me ask the grace to die before the evil commences? It seems to me, truly, that I am altogether incapable of doing good. Ask the good God, and I am confident He will speak to you in my favor. His Grace Mgr. De la Croix told me to write to our Mother, and ask her to favor him by sending a Sister capable of teaching grammar, geography, and the higher mathematics. The people hold the sciences in high estimation in this city. I beg you to continue the interest you took in our new establishment. We beg this favor for ourselves, still more for the Bishop of Gap."

This message was the means through which he could send her a lesson of humility, in which she found little encouragement.

"I will certainly consider your request for another Sister, and mention it to Mother St. Benedict; but I do not think it can be granted at once, since they are much embarrassed for Sisters at Belley and other missions. But have patience; delay will do no injury. The Jesuits make a year's novitiate, during which time they do not study, but occupy themselves solely with a desire to become worthy religious. Employ two or three months in forming your postulants to virtue. You may in the interval have them receive preparatory lessons. Your two Sisters know enough. It is not always those who are most learned that make the best teachers;- experience is needed as well as science. However, this is not a refusal; let it be an occasion for the practice of patience, and to recall a little of the spirit of humility and self-sacrifice, which I very much desire to revive in Mother St. Joseph, whose self-love, under the appearance of zeal, must be extinguished little by little. Be penetrated with these sentiments, and you will be more tranquil about the success of your mission and your labors. Obedience, which sent you, must now quiet you."

The comfort of the orphans and the old people whom she had left in the House of Providence at Belley was always a source of anxiety to her. He wrote to her in the same letter:

"The orphans are well cared for, and the old people have all their wants supplied. I trust, God willing, that everything will be gradually arranged. I recommend you to make an inventory of all you left in the house."

She retained in effect the ownership and administration of the goods of Providence, according to the will of the donor. Father

Girard, secretary of the bishop, to whom she had given, at Lyons, on the 22d of December, the power of attorney, administered in her name, and gave her an account of his administration. She mentioned also in her letter to Mgr. Devie that to a holy ecclesiastic, before going on a projected mission among strangers, was made known by revelation her vow to go to the Indies. He had come to Gap to introduce some postulants, to calm her fears, and allow her to continue to speak to our Lord in prayer, as she had ordinarily done. Surprised on learning that he knew of her vow and of her interior trials, she had conversed with him half an hour. She asked Mgr. Devie to impose a penance on her if she had done wrong. The bishop in his reply limited himself to asking the name of the priest and of what parish he had charge.

After a few months, the rarefied air of the Alps visibly impaired the previously declining health of Mother St. Joseph. This, joined to the efforts she imposed on herself to conquer her sadness and her fears, rendered her situation almost intolerable. Nevertheless, her virtue made her surmount all these difficulties, and, so great was the zeal and activity she displayed, no one suspected her sufferings.

The novitiate was opened on the arrival of. the Sisters. The month of March following the house was vacated, and in September of the same year a novitiate having thirty postulants was begun, and classes were organized and a large academy opened, into which pupils flocked in numbers. Mgr. Devie was then at Gap, near Mgr. De la Croix, and he came at the close of a retreat to give the habit to a number of postulants, and receive the vows of several novices. The venerable bishop could not restrain his tears on seeing so quickly flourish in the midst of the Alps a branch of the Congregation of St. Joseph, which he considered as one of the greatest works of his episcopate. His presence, his counsels, and his conversations, notwithstanding the reproaches usually attending them were also for the worthy superior a source of the greatest consolation.

CHAPTER XXVI.

CONVERSION OF TWO YOUNG GIRLS AT MARSEILLES.

DURING her stay at Gap Mother St. Joseph did not concentrate the exercise of her charity on the interior of her convent. Her pure soul cherished the deepest pity for the unhappy victims of crime, and she applied herself to convert them, and in the first years of her stay at Gap she had the good-fortune to bring about the repentance of two young girls in a house at Marseilles. One of them, whose dissolute life had been a scandal to every one, experienced great regret for the determination to which she had been influenced, and she resolved to take Mother St. Joseph's life. The means were all prepared, when an interior warning showed the Mother the danger by which she was threatened, and she managed to prevent the execution of the design. At Marseilles she had great trouble in having the girl received into the House of Reformation, because her appearance showed the violence of her character. At times she was the cause of great trouble and disturbance to her companions; but Mother St. Joseph prayed constantly for her, and at last grace triumphed, a sincere repentance took possession of her heart, and her last years were as edifying as her first had been scandalous.

She also visited the prisoners. In one of her visits she was struck by the calm resignation of one of the prisoners, named Nicholas B——. He was condemned in 1837 by the Court of Assizes to the life of a galley-slave, on a charge of counterfeiting; but the king commuted his punishment to twenty years' hard labor. On her first visit to this convict all her endeavors to open a conversation on religious truths were in vain; however, she understood that the obstacle existed more on account of absolute ignorance than of opposition, and she promised to bring him next day a book which would kill the tedious monotony of prison life. She had a catechism compiled by Mgr. Devie, and illustrated by a great number of engravings. The prisoner examined these with interest, and asked several questions, which gave her the opportunity of explaining successively all the truths of religion. This man, though baptized, had never performed one act of religion. Mother St. Joseph's words penetrated his soul like a refreshing dew, and developed there all the noble sentiments inspired by religion. He had an eager desire to listen to his pious instructress, and she, on her part, despite her labors and sufferings, did not let one day pass without visiting her dear prisoner. Time was pressing; for, once doomed to the galleys, the condemned might at any moment be removed from the prison. When sufficiently prepared for the reception of the most blessed Sacrament, he approached the holy table with sentiments of fervor and gratitude. He thanked God for His mercy and love, made manifest towards him by His willingness to descend into a heart deserving only the contempt of every one. He also thanked Him for inspiring the good religious to exercise her self-sacrificing charity in his behalf.

Mother St. Joseph resolved on a great undertaking. The 9th of March, 1838, she sent a petition to the king, asking pardon for her spiritual son. "This unfortunate young man," she wrote, "is guilty because he never knew the difference between right and wrong. Since he became instructed in religion he is not the same person. His truly touching example of resignation, repentance, mildness, and the good resolutions he made, have excited the admiration, and almost the respect, of his unfortunate companions, as well as the people of Gap. Sire, complete your work. Imitate the conduct of your divine Master, of whose power on earth you exercise a part. Pardon fully the converted one. Restore to society him who is become worthy, and by his sincere repentance covered his iniquities." In conclusion she promised to raise her protégée above want, and gave assurance of his perseverance in good. After a few weeks she received a letter from the Minister of Justice, announcing the penalty had been reduced to eighteen months. She hastened to convey the good news to the prisoner. Unable to thank her in words, he attempted to kiss her hands; but she prevented him, saying: "My son, thank God; remember that the grace of conversion is far greater than the favor you have now received. Eighteen months will see you leave the prison; but without the mercy of God, who gave you repentance, you would never have been released from the prison of eternal torments." While young B—— was still in the prison of Gap, two assassins were brought there, who only awaited the day of execution. They had killed a great number of persons, and they related that towards the close of their career, when they let a day pass without shedding human blood, they killed the first beast they met, so as to see the color of blood. Several times after their arrest they broke their chains and perpetrated new murders. As they passed before the door of the cell that contained B——, he said to them: "If you wish to find agreeable chains, make application to Mother St. Joseph." Confiding in the words of a companion in misfortune, they asked for the Mother; but the jailer would not allow her entrance into their dungeon, as he had strict orders not to admit any one. She then had recourse to the Prefect of Gap, who, yielding to her reiterated importunities, at last permitted her to visit the two prisoners, but only on condition that she be accompanied by an escort of soldiers. The two men were under the impression that the woman of whom they had heard was a sorceress. As soon as she entered they told her they would disclose to her where they had hidden a wealth of gold, and allow her its possession, if she would impart to them the secret and sweeten their sufferings. "Certainly," she said, "I will give you my secret, and will relieve you; but before doing so, I have many things to ask you and to teach you. Have you been baptized? And do you know how to make the sign of the cross?" Neither of them knew how to make the sign of the cross, but one of them believed that he had been baptized. On the second day she brought them a catechism similar to the one given her former protégé, and instructed them in the truths of which they read. So as to have sufficient time to instruct them fully, she obtained a reprieve of forty days for them. As the truths of religion penetrated their hearts, their ferocious characters softened and even their features underwent a marked change; and the soldiers unconsciously laid down their arms and listened quietly to the instructions of the devoted religious. When the two convicts were sufficiently instructed, they were conditionally baptized. They made their confession with sentiments of sincere sorrow, and received Holy Communion with feelings of deepest joy and lowly humility. Mother St. Joseph was between the two, and they kept as close as possible to her, persuaded that the fervor of her dispositions would enter into them, and that the Saviour Jesus would descend into their souls more willingly because of the sanctity of her in whose company they were. These sentiments of humble repentance are agreeable to God, who has promised: "If the sinner do penance, I will no longer remember his sins." He regarded only their present dispositions, and in the Communion He heaped upon them an abundance of ineffable graces.

Mgr. de la Croix gave them the sacrament of confirmation. When they received the Holy Ghost, their hearts, animated by a superhuman courage, conceived a desire for the day of their public expiation, in order that they might fully offer the sacrifice of their lives to the God whom they had outraged by their crimes. On the day of the execution the barber by accident cut off a piece of the ear of one of the condemned. He did not perceive what he had done until the flow of blood told of the existence of the wound. The patient had not said a word, and replied to the pardon asked by the man: "Do not be troubled, sir; the good God will receive me as well with one ear as with two." He then embraced him who in a few moments would be obliged to take his life. Mother St. Joseph went to Chamberry to avoid a possibility of being present at the execution. She prayed incessantly for them, and all the efforts of Sister St. Wilfrid, who accompanied her, were fruitless to distract her thoughts from them for even a moment. On the day of the execution, at half-past ten o'clock A.M., she experienced a lively emotion of joy on seeing the souls of the condemned raised to heaven. She remarked to the Sister: "The justice of man is satisfied, and that of God is overcome by His mercy. My dear prisoners are in heaven." The Sister said that the execution was not to take place until noon; but on their return they learned that for some special reason the time had been advanced an hour and a half.

Some months afterwards a messenger came to tell her that a sick soldier had for several days been requesting to see her. She was sick at the time, but she sent for a carriage, and went immediately to the hospital. On speaking to the sick man she learned that he despaired of salvation. He was one of the guard who had accompanied her to the dungeon of the assassins, and had listened attentively to her instructions, being convinced of the truth of all she taught; but the conviction only increased his hopelessness.

"Why do you thus despair, my son? How great soever be your crimes, God wants only repentance. The blood of

Jesus Christ, whose merits will be applied to you in the sacraments, will wash out your sins. All that is necessary for you is to prepare to receive the sacrament of penance."

"But I cannot make my confession, Mother, when I am not a Catholic."

"Well, my son, you can soon be a Catholic; for already you are one at heart."

The poor soldier was not aware that becoming a Catholic rested with himself. However, when disabused of this idea, he gladly abjured his error, received the sacraments, and died some days afterwards in sentiments of a lively faith and an entire confidence in the mercy of God.

CHAPTER XXVII.

FOUNDATION OF REMOLLEN.

IN the performance of all these acts of charity Mother St. Joseph did not neglect her principal work—the spiritual and temporal progress of her congregation. The novices continued to present themselves in great numbers, and in the month of October, 1838, the Mother founded a new house in one of the parishes of the diocese, called Remollen.

The vocation of the young novices was frequently accompanied by remarkable and extraordinary circumstances.

One of them was about to be married. The betrothal had been given and the contract signed. The night following the Blessed Virgin appeared to her in a dream, and commanded her to choose the religious life, at the same time telling her to enter at Gap, where the Sisters had recently arrived. On the following day the young betrothed made her dream known to her parents, who placed no opposition to the will of God. They went immediately to Gap, to relate the whole to Mother St. Joseph, and to present their daughter, who became a fervent religious.

Another postulant fainted on seeing the Mother, and she could not for a long time look at her without turning pale and trembling. The Mother having asked why her presence produced this effect, the young girl replied: "For a long time I desired to become a religious, and presented myself to two communities, but was refused admission for want of a dowry. I keenly felt this rejection, and complained to our Lord for having created in me a desire to quit the world without giving me the means to fulfil this desire, when one night I saw Him in a dream, and he assured me that my wish was about to be realized. Pointing to a religious, He said: 'Look at your Mother; she will receive you, notwithstanding your poverty.' After a few days, our Lord appeared to me again, and said that the Mother who would receive me had arrived at Gap. I told all to the curé of my parish, who gave me a letter for you. On my arrival in the city I enquired for the Sisters who had come recently, and was directed here. On seeing you I immediately recognized the Sister that had been shown me in my dream."

"My child," said Mother St. Joseph, "these are only woman's imaginings. Pay no attention to them, and do not mention them, or persons will look upon you as a visionary."

The girl was received as a lay Sister, and she lived a fervent life, edifying all by her amiability of manner, her humility, mortification, and diligence.

Shortly after her arrival at Gap, Mother St. Joseph noticed a young person named Louise Guttin, who was employed as governess in a certain family. In her conversation she took occasion to tell her that she believed she had a religious vocation. Louise answered that for years she had entertained a great desire to consecrate herself to God; but, being the eldest of four orphans, she could not bring herself to leave her younger sisters dependent on strangers. One of them was a cripple, and had been bedridden for several years. Mother St. Joseph promised to attend to the welfare of the two healthy girls, and to take charge herself of the invalid. During the ensuing vacation Louise went to visit her sisters, and she often spoke to them of the great charity of Mother St. Joseph and her power with God.

At mention of the wonderful cures obtained through her prayers, the sick girl, Alexandrine, felt an indefinable interior agitation, and she believed that the end of her sufferings approached.

Towards the close of vacation Louise received a letter from Mother St. Joseph, telling her to return to Gap and bring her afflicted sister with her. Louise obeyed the wish, and arrived at Gap on the 5th of November, 1838.

The fatigue of the journey considerably weakened the young girl, but the affectionate welcome given her wrought a change for the better.

Mother St. Joseph embraced her, and said: "At last, my child, I am permitted to greet you. It is now twenty years since our Lord promised you to me, and you shall never leave me."

She kept her in her own room, and bestowed on her the most tender and assiduous care.

On the Feast of the Immaculate Conception she commenced a novena in honor of the Blessed Virgin, and promised, on the part of the young girl, that if her recovery were granted she would become a religious under the name of Mary of the Immaculate Conception. Alexandrine had no great hope, but Mother St. Joseph assured her that God wanted her for Himself, and He would accomplish His design in her regard. This assurance awakened her confidence, and her joy was unbounded. She united her intention and prayers with Mother St. Joseph, and at that time was formed a bond of friendship that united these two hearts until death suspended for a time their intimate union. On the 8th of December Alexandrine was so much restored in health and strength as to be able to follow the exercises of the community and commence her postulate. The Sisters were very much dissatisfied with the reception of this subject, whom they considered a burden to the congregation, and towards whom the Mother manifested too great an attachment; and the superior of the house joined the Sisters in opposing the reception. Mgr. Devie, to whom Mother St. Joseph submitted all her proceedings, wrote her to dismiss this postulant, and to follow the advice of the superior and the Sisters in the admission of subjects. But, relying on the designs of God, she resisted the will of the bishop, and obtained permission from Mgr. de la Croix to have the girl received. He gave the holy habit to Alexandrine on the 19th of May, with the name Mary of the Immaculate Conception. Her sister received the habit at the same time, under the name of Sister de Chantal. She was the third Superior-General of Gap, and filled this office from 1842 until her death, in 1856.

In the first walk for recreation after the reception of May the Mother led the

Sisters up the side of a neighboring mountain. They were supplied with mules, in case of necessity for their use It was proposed to visit a poor shepherd who was said to be a great servant of God. The road to his dwelling was over the worst passes on the mountain, and the Sisters who were not able to climb the ascent easily were allotted mules. The one assigned to Sister Immaculate Conception became frightened and threw her. She held on to the reins, and was dragged over the rocks and briers, until every moment she expected death. When the mule was caught, the Sisters feared to find Sister Immaculate Conception dead. Mother St. Joseph had constantly repeated: "St. Michael the Archangel, save her!"

On approaching where she lay she said: "My child, all is possible to those whose faith is firm. Do not doubt St. Michael will cure you. Stand up!"

The Sister obeyed, and neither bruise nor wound was apparent. She felt no pain, nor was there any trace of the accident. The Sister herself related this fact. Divine Providence thus prepared and protected in a weak novice, who seemed destined to a short life, one who in time aided Mother St. Joseph in all her foundations, and kept alive her spirit and prosecuted her works long after her soul had gone to God.

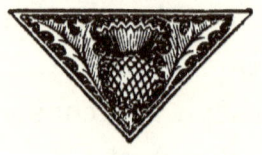

CHAPTER XXVIII.

NEW FOUNDATIONS.

EARLY in 1839 Mother St. Joseph was afflicted with paralysis of the right arm. The necessity of having a Sister constantly with her to assist her in all she did was no small occasion for constant violence to her nature. The malady increased after the reception on May 19, and she decided to spend a month at the baths at Aix. She went to Belley, accompanied by her young novice, to celebrate the feast of St. Anthelme, June 26. Mgr. Devie was pleased to see her. The prefect of the city, the magistrates, the principal families of Belley, and a multitude of other persons came to visit her. Her presence awakened a remembrance of all the good she had done in the city, and renewed the feelings of gratitude which persons had preserved towards her.

A distinguished physician of Paris, who was then at Belley, examined her arm. Believing it to contain a carious bone, he said an amputation was necessary, and that the baths would only aggravate the evil. Bishop Devie was in favor of her going to Aix, in the hope that, even if her arm were not relieved, the general state of her health would be improved. To do away with all indecision, Mother St. Joseph went to the Chapel of St. Anthelme, and besought the saint to show by a sign which course she should pursue. Her faith was rewarded and the desired sign given. She accordingly went to Aix, and met there several Sisters of St. Joseph from Lyons, among whom was the venerable Mother St. John, then in her eighty-first year. This holy religious was the first superior-general of the Sisters of St. Joseph. Her character combined a correct judgment, an amiable simplicity, goodness without parallel, and an angelic piety. She was a living exemplar of the rules of her order.

Mother St. Joseph, perceiving some slight difference in the form and size of the capes worn by Mother St. John and herself, took a pattern from the Rev. Mother's, so that in the congregation the simple and modest habit of the old religious, as well as their spirit, should be exactly maintained.

Notwithstanding the predictions to the contrary, the waters at Aix restored Mother St. Joseph the use of her arm, and worked a marked improvement in her health. She returned to Gap the 2d of August, 1839. God restored the strength of her constitution to sustain her through the sad trials that awaited her.

In 1840 she made two new foundations, at Abries and Veynes, but her uneasiness was increased by the news given her in the month of January by M. Depery of the probable departure of Bishop de la Croix. She was also very much afflicted at the death of a professed Sister whom she had brought from Belley, and of a young novice. Sister St. Wilfrid, superior of the hospital at Gap from August, 1839, died in March, 1840. After having caused Mother St. Joseph great trouble, both at Belley and at Gap, she at last corrected herself, and began to practise in earnest the virtues necessary for a religious. She had a tender devotion to the souls in purgatory; great exactitude in her religious exercises; an admirable zeal and a particular gift to prepare children for their first communion; also, to inspire in them a horror of sin and great charity for the poor. On her death-bed she said to the Sisters assembled around her: "Whatever be your faults, never be discouraged. You can correct them as well as I have corrected mine; with openness of heart, time, and a good will, persons can accomplish all things." Her death caused universal mourning in the city. Mother St. Joseph was suffering from pneumonia when the news of the death was brought her, and she was painfully affected. The young novice who died was Sister St. Stanislaus. Her patience, humility, and fervor made her example useful to the Sisters. She died June 11, 1840. Later in the month the Mother went to celebrate the Feast of St. Anthelme at Belley, whence she returned to Aix to take the baths, as in the preceding year. On the 29th of July she received a letter from Bishop de la Croix, announcing his departure from Gap to take charge of the archbishopric of Auch. She herself returned to Gap August 2, 1840, and found the community most unfavorably disposed towards her. Her absence and the departure of Bishop de la Croix, in giving the vicar-general more moral authority as superior and confessor, had greatly lessened her own authority. After having asked the assistance of Heaven, she did her best to show goodness and affection for all the Sisters, speaking privately and separately to those who seemed estranged from the others; but her words were unheeded, and her remonstrances no more attended to than her encouragements. She expected a great good from the coming retreat to be made in September; but the religious who gave it, instead of confining himself to explanations on the great truths of religion that would bring peace to souls and direct their aspirations to heaven, took part in the interior difficulties of the house, praised the authority of the director, whose orders, he said, were always to be obeyed before those of the superior. He went still further, and allowed several Sisters to leave the congregation, and told them they were called by God to enter the Convent of the Ladies of the Sacred Heart. Mother St. Joseph wrote on the 1st of October to Bishop de la Croix, to inform him of the state of affairs and ask his advice. The prelate replied on the 8th of October, giving words of encouragement, telling her to endure persecution for God's love, and to refer the matter to Bishop Devie, who, perhaps, was aware of the cause of dissatisfaction, and to be subject to his decision. She had already written to the latter for permission to go and see him at Belley, and, having obtained it, she left Gap with Sister Immaculate Conception on the 12th of October, 1840, while the community were in the country. She should never have returned to the city where she had suffered so intensely in body and soul. She was diversely judged there, but she left evident marks of her spirit and the fruits of her good works in the spiritual progress that infallibly characterizes the servants of God. Three years had sufficed, in the midst of contradictions of all kinds, for a work so difficult as the foundation of a religious congregation. When she left Gap, the congregation numbered eight houses, forty-five Sisters and novices, and twelve postulants.

CHAPTER XXIX.

MOTHER ST. JOSEPH GOES TO BORDEAUX.

MOTHER ST. JOSEPH, on arriving at Belley, accompanied by Sister Immaculate Conception, was received less affectionately than ordinarily by Bishop Devie, and this coldness was a most sensible blow to her soul, already sadly depressed. He gave her for examination a petition that had been sent from Gap, and which contained sixteen charges against her administration; among others, that of depriving the Sisters of necessaries to gratify her avarice. The Bishop knew his spiritual daughter too well not to be able to separate in these reproaches the charges having foundation from those which were but the echo of discontented and angry minds; but the reading of the petition was not the less a source of the deepest humiliation to her. He blamed above all what he called her prejudice against Sister Mary Gertrude and against the superior of the house, and also her want of firmness in the case of two novices and one professed whom she had dismissed. He added that she should not consider herself discharged from the mission at Gap, and that she should return there after the installation of a new bishop. The next day he heard the confession of the two Sisters, gave them Holy Communion during Mass, and wished Mother St. Joseph to receive Holy Communion every day, as she had ordinarily done.

During the three years that had intervened since she left Belley, the severe climate of the Alps and the frequent sickness to which she was subject had completely shattered her constitution. On the other hand, the difficulties of administration, the continual restraint and violence imposed on herself to overcome all her repugnances, and show exteriorly the activity necessary to the performance of such works as the foundation, had, as it were, lessened her moral energy. The welcome received at Belley was calculated to depress her spirits. Moreover, the people no longer recognized the Mother St. Joseph of old; her readiness to reply, her clear decisions, her firm will, were all of the past. She would scarcely speak to any one who came to visit her. When advice was asked of her, she would answer: "I do not know what I would do; examine the matter and decide for yourself." Besides, she almost entirely lost her memory, and in fact never fully recovered this faculty; for in the course of her life she frequently related facts of recent occurrence in an incorrect way. In the convent her daughters reminded her of the real facts; but when alone with strangers, or when accompanied by a Sister too timid to speak, this fault of memory was more than once the occasion for persons to suppose her too loose in her narration of facts. Sister Immaculate Conception, ignorant of what had occurred at Belley, could not direct her superior in the way of truth, and this brought new humiliations on her. At Belley, where she had a few years previously received expressions of the greatest respect and gratitude, she was not wanted by the people, who complained and blamed at the same time. Her visions, her agitated manner, her unfounded prejudices, had, they said, forced her to leave Gap; there was no truth in her words, and she contradicted herself at every instant. Her weakened faculties left nothing to be desired for her but a peaceful death in some remote house of the order. Her friends, Father Colletta and Father Depery, Vicar-General of Belley, were her only support. The venerable Bishop of Belley believed her mind deranged, and he gave up the intention of sending her back to Gap, but did not replace her at the head of the congregation at Belley. One day, while at prayer in the chapel, she felt herself forced to go and tell the bishop not to send Father Depery to engage a place for her at the insane asylum. She obeyed the impulse much against the will of her companion. When she was introduced, the bishop was in conversation with Father Depery. Mother St. Joseph fell on her knees and said to him: "Bishop, I come on the part of my good Master to say to you that I am not insane, and to beg you to countermand the order given to Father Depery." The bishop, much astonished, replied: "'Tis well; I do not believe that you are insane, but I have thought that a course of treatment followed in one of these asylums would be useful to you." It was in the midst of this deep melancholy that the ultimate designs of Providence in regard to Mother St. Joseph commenced to manifest themselves.

This truly extraordinary woman, who had already signalized herself by works stamped with the seal of charity and of faith, was then regarded by her superiors as a useless instrument, worn out and unfit to longer labor in the service of God. She herself was also of the same opinion; but He who exalts the humble chose this moment to have her undertake the principal work of her life. She had made known to her nephew her arrival at Belley, and her intention to spend there, at least, the time necessary for the restoration of her health. Father Montcenis had been at Bordeaux for two years, and several times the archbishop had expressed a desire to have Mother St. Joseph found a novitiate of her order in his diocese. The circumstances appeared favorable, and he hastened to anticipate the wishes of Archbishop Donnet, who charged him to write to his aunt that, if she could come to Bordeaux, a home and necessary furniture would be immediately placed at her disposal. This news surprised Mother St. Joseph, and made a deep impression on her, as it confirmed all her former predictions. She showed her nephew's letter to Father Depery, who saw in it a manifestation of Providence, and he undertook to write to Archbishop Donnet, saying he would correspond with Bishop Devie, then at Bourg, concerning the departure of Mother St. Joseph. On the 6th of November Archbishop Donnet replied: "You are exceeding kind, my dear Father Depery; our poor villages are in a most abandoned condition, so much so that you cannot form even an idea of the reality Except in the cities of Bordeaux, Libourne, and of Reole, many persons have never seen a religious costume. All the young children are attending the established schools taught by laics. Besides, after the three missionary houses I have erected, I desire nothing more than a mother-house of the Sisters of St. Joseph to supply the wants of our cities and villages. Allow the good Mother St. Joseph, whom I have known for a long time, to come to us as soon as she can. If she can bring a colony of three or four Sisters with her, matters could be all the better arranged." The reading of this letter inflamed the zeal of Mother St. Joseph. She saw much good to be done and a vast field to cultivate, and she prayed Father Depery to solicit the necessary authorization. On the 12th of November she wrote to Archbishop Donnet, to render him an account of her proceedings, and informed him of her acceptance in these terms: "I see in your proposition the will of God, and am resolved to embrace it; but I will bring you only zeal and devotedness. I have more courage than health, more organization than learning, and am rich in corporal and spiritual miseries; but I am confident in Him who chooses weak instruments to accomplish great things. I am accustomed to see that His divine arm is powerful, and that all can place themselves under His protection without fear of either the world or hell. After God I rely on you, whose virtues and eminent holiness I well know." How ever, this brief period of courage was succeeded by long hours of sadness and fear. She imagined that it was only an illusion of the demon that had inspired her with the idea of undertaking this most important work in the state of weakness to which she was reduced. She said to her young companion: "I have neither health, talents, nor the virtues necessary for it. My task is finished. Instead of being useful to religion or the souls of others, I may promote only their perdition. You saw how matters went on at Gap towards the last." The Sister endeavored to reanimate her courage: "What signifies health? God can restore it to you, if he wishes. Besides, whether you be weak or in the enjoyment of robust health, He knows well how to make you serve His designs." Then replied the good Mother: "Let us pray and say from the depths of our hearts, 'Thy will be done on earth as it is in heaven.'" Another time the thought of St. Andrew saluting with joy the instrument of his torture reanimated her courage, and she said with the apostle: "O good cross! come, that I may embrace you."

Bishop Devie was in no hurry to give the permission asked by his vicar-general. He desired Mother St. Joseph to make over to the congregation at Bourg the titles and the revenue of the Goux inheritance. But, in acceding to his wish, she would act in direct opposition to her conscience; consequently, she absolutely refused. In her first transaction with M. Goux he had not the happiness of professing the true faith. He gave the bequest to this woman, whom he admired on account of her devotedness and incomparable charity, although she was a religious. He never intended to give to the congregation, and his sentiments on this point never underwent a change, even when he embraced the faith and practices of a Christian. The conditions of his will imposed the administration and personal ownership on Mother St. Joseph, and they were accepted with the consent and approbation of Bishop Devie. These conditions she had always fulfilled, both at Belley and at Gap, either herself or through an attorney. She had always sold, exchanged, and administered the goods left by M. Goux, without rendering an account to any one. It was natural that she should wish to continue the administration at Bordeaux as she had at Gap. Bishop Devie, on the contrary, exacted that she should relinquish her claims in favor of the congregation at Bourg. This was directly opposed to the intention of the donor and to the rights of personal property, without any security. Moreover, he himself had approved the transfer, and it was made sacred by a solemn judgment. Nevertheless, the bishop was immovable in his opinion. He would consent to her departure only on this condition. Mother St. Joseph, beset by these annoyances and struggles, was also constrained by a desire to leave for Bordeaux with the blessing of her superiors; and at the advice of Fathers Depery and Colletta, who told her that, after all, Bishop Devie, as her bishop and her director, was responsible before God for what he obliged her to do, she finished by granting and signing all he required of her.

The 23d of the same month Bishop Devie wrote to her and gave her leave to go to Bordeaux. "I regret," he added, "that I am not at Belley to give my blessing to yourself and companion; but I freely confer it from here, and pray the Almighty to assist you in all your enterprises."

On December 1 the venerable Mother St. Benedict, superior-general at Bourg, wrote to her to express her sympathy in all her troubles at Gap and the hopes she entertained for the success of her new enterprise. "I feel," she said, "as well as all the congregation, grateful for what you have done for us while you were with us. I pray you, good Mother, to believe, in all the sincerity of my heart, we cannot see you leave without great sorrow, and at this moment our hearts are grieved at the loss of one who labored long and generously among us. Were it not for the hope that you will find peace, content, and full appreciation in your new home, and promote the glory of God and the good of souls, our grief would indeed be most bitter."

She also told her that she would send two Sisters to accompany her to Bordeaux —Sisters St. Bridget and St. Paul, the latter then superior of the establishment at Champagne.

CHAPTER XXX.

MOTHER ST. JOSEPH ESTABLISHES HER ORDER AT BARSAC.

THE Diocese of Bordeaux is the most extensive and one of the most important in France. It contains a population of nearly seven hundred thousand, divided into five hundred and forty-seven parishes. Two great bishops, both of whom were missionaries and confessors of the faith—Bishop Avian and Cardinal Cheverus—had occupied the see after the Revolution, when divine Providence called to it, in 1836, a bishop, also a missionary, who displayed an incomparable zeal and facility for organization. On the arrival of the new bishop one hundred and ninety-seven churches were deprived of their parochial titles, and the congregations were obliged to assemble at the nearest district; and eighty-two parishes were without pastors. Many of the churches were in so ruinous a condition that they were unsafe and in danger of falling. The diocese counted twenty-eight parochial residences, many of which were unoccupied. Religious communities were established in the principal cities, and attended to the education of youth; but the parishes and the villages were deprived of these aids, the offices were not sung, and the public devotions every Sunday were limited to one Low Mass, rarely followed by Vespers. One priest had two, three, sometimes four, churches to attend. Many of the members of the clergy were strangers in the place, and had come from Spain, Ireland, Corsica, and various dioceses of France. Since 1837 one hundred and five parish chapels and nineteen private chapels had been erected, eighty-six titles of parish residences obtained, one hundred and thirty-four new churches constructed, and more than two hundred repaired or almost renovated. Thirteen religious orders were established, applying themselves to the duties of instructing youth; and thirty-two congregations of women, making in the diocese two hundred and thirty houses affording the benefit of a Christian and religious education. The Christian and the Marianite Brothers, also the Brothers of Lavala de Ploermel, had opened schools in thirty-seven country districts.

This great development of Catholic institutions, worthy the best age of the church, was but in its beginning when Archbishop Donnet called Mother St. Joseph to take a part that, humanly speaking, had nothing to indicate the admirable proportions which it would one day attain.

Mother St. Joseph left Belley with Sister Conception and Sister Bridget, a professed lay Sister whom Mother St. Benedict had sent. Sister St. Paul would join them at Bordeaux a little later

The last visit she made at Belley to the most blessed Sacrament was unusually long. She could not leave without recommending to her divine Master the souls of those she loved at Belley. She thanked Him for the great favors He had bestowed upon her in that city, and, above all, for the sorrows of the last weeks, the salutary bitterness of which had aided to detach her from all terrestrial affections. The three Sisters spent Sunday, the 6th of December, at Lyons, and Mother St. Joseph remained nearly all day at the feet of Our Lady of Fourvières. In this cradle of her religious vocation she felt a heavenly calm revive in her heart. She seemed to behold a multitude of young virgins come at the call of God to range themselves under her guidance, and to apply themselves with ardor to the Christian instruction of children. Abundant tears coursed from her eyes, and she said to the Blessed Virgin: "Choose them yourself, O Mary! for they are to be worthy spouses of your Son; be their mother in my place. I will be your servant, and will act exteriorly, while you will operate in their souls."

While at Lyons the Mother received a letter of encouragement from Father Colletta, whom she had gone to see before leaving Belley. He knew all her apprehensions, and said to her: "Because you fear yourself, you are more fit to promote the works of God; regard yourself in His hands as the rod in the hands of Moses. A rod always takes the direction given it by the hand; do you take care to give it a right direction. Nothing is easier than to spoil the work of God; and fear of spoiling this is a great grace." He then spoke of the good her visit had done him; it revived his soul, and he felt himself forced to think more of God. "Since your visit," he said, "I have more strength and courage, and occupy myself more with thoughts of death. I regard the happy effects that your words produced on me as an extraordinary grace, all the more precious because it is rare."

Travel from Lyons to Bordeaux then occupied three days, and was tiresome in that severe season; but the Mother seemed to recover new life, resumed her old lively, spirited, and engaging manner of conversation, and made the route agreeable to her companions, and even to the other travellers. She frequently expressed to the latter a desire to pray in a loud voice with the Sisters; and they not only acceded to this desire, but nearly all piously joined in the prayers.

On Thursday, the 10th of December, 1840, the colony of the future Congregation of St. Joseph arrived at Bordeaux. When the Mother perceived the roof of the cathedral, she saluted the angel guardians of all the inhabitants, and prayed to her own angel to go and in her name visit our Saviour in all the sanctuaries of that opulent city. She went to the community of Maria Theresa by way of Noyers, and the next day she went to receive the archbishop's blessing. The prelate welcomed her with marks of the most touching goodness. He spoke of the good to be done in his vast diocese, and the plans he meditated, in a way that filled her with enthusiasm. She interiorly thanked God for having called her to labor under the direction of an all-apostolic soul, whose ardor so well corresponded with the sentiments that animated her own.

The ladies of Maria Theresa received the new Sisters with much cordiality; the superior, Madame St. Stanislaus, asked Mother St. Joseph to give conferences to the Sisters, and she immediately complied, being always willing and anxious to speak of God or of His divine service. She then discoursed on obedience, regularity, and holy charity, and her words deeply impressed the Sisters. After a few days the archbishop sent for her to offer a foundation for an establishment at Barsac, a small village of two thousand souls eleven miles distant from Bordeaux. This proposition was as a lightning-flash to the pious foundress. For several weeks her ardent soul drew in her meditation a work whose basis would be capable of responding to the wants of the extensive diocese. She had counted on a house at Bordeaux, and felt sure of resources proportionate to the importance of the work. Placed all at once in presence of the reality, it seemed her imagination and her heart had been the play of day-dreams, and that the first ray of joy had vanished. Nevertheless, accustomed to place reliance in divine Providence, she asked permission to reflect, and she went to Barsac on Saturday, 19th of December

The parish priest of the place, Father Labonne, had a heart of gold under a rude and even coarse manner. He received the Sisters with great cordiality, and one of the best families of the city offered them a kind hospitality. The worthy priest with his vicar retired for some time to a small building near the church, and reserved the parochial residence as a lodging for the new religious. It was a one-story cottage, composed of three rooms, a cabinet, and a kitchen; to this was attached a yard and a garden. The house was empty. M. Labonne offered four hundred and fifty francs to purchase the most necessary furniture. This small establishment, in a remote village, was far from realizing the first hopes of Mother St. Joseph; but convinced by her own experience that the works of God are always humble and obscure in the beginning, she accepted without more hesitation the offer of the priest at Barsac.

On Sunday, after Vespers, the Sisters found in the sacristy a choir of young girls who were practising the psalms. The Mother complimented them on their manner of singing, and said a few words on the happiness of serving God and the vanity of worldly pleasures. The priest took this occasion to single out a young person, Mademoiselle Désire Destanque, who was, he said, an incorrigible dancer, and thus the scandal of her companions, and deserving to be dismissed the choir. The young girl covered her face to hid her confusion; but the Mother, regarding her with eyes full of tears, took her by the arm, and drew her towards her, saying, "Come, my child, you are my first daughter." All the others smiled incredulously, the priest was astonished; but the words of the Mother were realized very soon after, and the wild young girl became a holy religious.

On Monday morning the Sisters returned to the congregation of Maria Theresa, and during the day Mother St. Joseph made known to the archbishop her resolution to accept Barsac.

CHAPTER XXXI.

ARRIVAL OF SISTER ST. PAUL.

S soon as they arrived at Bordeaux, Sister Immaculate Conception commenced a retreat; and on Wednesday, 23d of December, Feast of St. Delphine, she made her profession in the Chapel of the Ladies of the Sacred Heart, at the hands of Mgr. Donnet. After Mass, he gave an instruction on the happiness of the religious life and the excellence of the vows of religion. He exhorted Mother St. Joseph to bear up against the privations and the trials inseparable to her foundation, and said to the assembly: "Consider these pious women who have crossed France at our appeal. I foresee that at this moment I plant in the midst of you the roots of a great tree. It is the grain of mustard-seed of the Gospel. I drop it into the earth; God will give it

growth, and one day in the not distant future you will see it cover my diocese with its branches."

These words afforded Mother St. Joseph great consolation. It seemed as if God had sent them to refresh her courage and reanimate her zeal.

On the following day, December 24, the Sisters left for Barsac, where they arrived the evening of the same day. The parochial residence of Barsac, destined to be the first convent of the new Congregation of St. Joseph, was what is called in the country a *chartreuse*—a cottage—that is to say, a small one-story house. It was fronted by a small yard; on one side was another more extensive ground covered with fig-trees, and on the other a spacious garden. Her first care was to establish great cleanliness in this house, which had been unoccupied for some time. A general scrubbing was needed. Always accustomed to give the example to her Sisters, she commenced the work herself; and, as she never did anything by halves, in washing the walls of the kitchen she discovered, above the chimney, an oil painting which the dust and the smoke had almost entirely effaced. She found, on cleansing it, that it represented the Holy Family.

The good Mother, who beheld in everything the hand of divine Providence, placed this picture in the chapel, and said to the Sisters: "It is not without a motive that this has been preserved in a place destined to be the cradle of a congregation consecrated to Jesus, Mary, and Joseph."

She had bought at Bordeaux a statue of St. Joseph, which she placed in the community room, near one of the Blessed Virgin, found in the presbytery. She went on her knees at the feet of these two images, and made a fervent prayer in a loud voice. She besought Mary and Joseph to bless all three, and all those who would place themselves under the banner of St. Joseph. She then laid at their feet the keys of the house, and, considering herself unworthy to be the foundress, she prayed them to be true superiors of the community, or else not to permit its establishment.

To have the chapel prepared as quickly as possible for the most Blessed Sacrament was the chief desire of the pious superior.

Boards covered with white calico made the frame-work of an altar that received the sacred stone; an old tabernacle belonging to the church at Barsac, and a little ciborium donated by the parish priest, formed all the furniture necessary; and on the 30th of December the pastor came, celebrated Holy Mass, and left the Blessed Sacrament in the temporary chapel. Mother St. Joseph could not contain her joy. She was near Jesus, and saw herself poor, as He was. At first the trunks, as on a previous mission, answered for chairs and table. The dishes and kitchen utensils were three iron pans, three plates, one soup-tureen, and an earthen bowl.

On Monday, January 4, the school was opened with only five children, but the number increased gradually, and on the 19th of March, the Feast of St. Joseph, the class numbered sixty little girls. The Mother helped Sister Conception to teach reading and writing, but herself exclusively taught the catechism. Her great happiness was to see herself surrounded by those dear little girls, and to speak to them of God. She often returned to the first question of the catechism: "Who created you and placed you in the world?" As she felt a lively gratitude for the goodness of God, who gave us being and life, and destined us to eternal glory, she transfused these principles into the hearts of the children. Then she added: "You ought to love the good God, my little friends; but to be able to love Him you must understand and know Him, and all this you will learn from the catechism. Listen, then, very attentively, and when you leave think of it and speak of it among yourselves, and you will see that, knowing the good God and loving him with all your heart, you will find no trouble in serving Him." The children were not only interested in what she said, but knowing instinctively how much she loved them, even the smallest among them were afflicted at the threat of not being allowed to go to catechism. She wished also to habituate the children to taste the happiness of prayer without fatiguing themselves by long exercises. When a little girl deserved punishment, she said: "My child, you have not been wise enough to-day to go to the chapel. If you do not promise to be better you must pray alone, and I will make the prayers with your companions." Often these simple words called forth many tears, and promises that were kept at least a day. Her zeal was not confined to children. She invited the young girls and women to meet at the convent on Sundays for an hour. As the word catechism might keep them away, she was careful not to give it that name. "She wished," she said, "to give them interesting reading, and to teach them the history of our holy religion." Her call was numerously responded to, and crowds came to hear the discourses given by Mother St. Joseph. The simplicity and animation of her words so much interested her audience, that a young girl without instruction easily recounted to the Mother each Sunday what she had heard on the preceding Sunday. In a short time the condition of the community was greatly improved.

On the 10th of January she wrote to one of her most generous friends, M. Pasquier, of Lyons. After detailing the state of the religious community, the greater part of this letter was consecrated to spiritual advice. She recommended to him above all interior prayer. "This sort of prayer dilates our hearts, elevates our souls, and makes us see God face to face, as our best friend and the most tender of fathers. It makes us consider ourselves as little children who go to their father with all their wants, without any exception. You will find an inexhaustible mine, a hidden treasure—graces for yourself and graces for others. Pardon me for what I am about to remark, but I believe that you are wanting in amiability and kindness to your nieces. I wish that every one could say of you that if before your conversion you were amiable, you are since meek, and humble, and blessed with evenness of temper." A few days after receiving this letter, M. Pasquier replied, thanking her for her advice, and begging her acceptance of a chalice, a ciborium, and silver cruets. The Ladies of the Sacred Heart at Bordeaux sent two sets of altar linen at the same time.

The arrival of Sister St. Paul, on January 20, was a great encouragement to the good

Mother. This Sister had been for many years superior of a numerous community in the parish of Champagne, in the diocese of Belley. Her rare prudence, her meekness and charity, left nothing undone, and had drawn towards her the hearts of her religious, and won the affection and respect of the people. She lived near her aged parents, who had always cherished the consoling hope that their daughter would one day close their eyes in death. Nevertheless, when Mother St. Benedict made known Mother St. Joseph's request for Sisters, and left her free to accompany her or to remain, she decided on the first course without a moment's hesitation, and immediately made all necessary preparations for her departure, in spite of the deep sadness of those who surrounded her. The season was rigorous, and a part of the roads of Bugey obstructed by snow, and she did not reach Barsac until after a sixteen days' journey; but all was forgotten when she met Mother St. Joseph and placed herself anew under the direction of her who had presided at her first step in the religious life, and made upon her soul an ineffaceable impression. She shed tears of joy. Mother St. Joseph was not less happy. She admired the devotedness of her spiritual daughter, and believed she had now near her a soul solidly established in the practice of religious virtues. She intended to place Sister St. Paul in charge of a new house about to be established.

A fourth Sister was asked of Mother St. Benedict, but she wrote saying it was impossible to comply with this demand. After the inundation of 1840, which was attended with great material loss to the congregation, the epidemic had taken several Sisters, and the vacancies caused by their deaths had not yet been filled. This refusal painfully affected Mother St. Joseph; but she was still more afflicted to learn of the severe trials to which her dear community at Belley were subjected, and she showed the letter to Mgr. Donnet. The worthy archbishop immediately sent a check for five hundred francs to the venerable Mother St. Benedict, with some words of consolation and the expression of gratitude for having sent the Sisters to Barsac.

CHAPTER XXXII.

HER CARE OF THE SICK.

THE arrival of Sister St. Paul, by increasing the number of religious, allowed Mother St. Joseph to devote more attention to the sick and the poor. She was gifted with power to console them, to reanimate their failing courage, and to bring them to an entire conformity of their will to the Divine will. At the approach of death her first and greatest care was to prepare them for the worthy reception of the sacraments. Far from wearying them with useless conversations, she contrived means to alleviate their sufferings, and herself rendered them all the services their condition required. Her kindness knew no bounds. While performing these duties, she frequently repeated short ejaculations inspiring faith, hope, confidence, and love; and as these proceeded from her heart the patient was never insensible to them. She would not allow the sick to speak lest doing so would fatigue them, but said: "Unite yourself interiorly to the sentiments I repeat to the good God for you."

When the Holy Viaticum was brought to the dying she would accompany the priest, and induce as many persons as possible to be present. She saw that the room was in order, and recommended the walls and the furniture to be covered with white. Nothing was spared on her part to show the deepest respect for Jesus in His sacramental Presence. What afflicted her most was the solitude that reigned around the tabernacle, and the indifference of the people towards frequenting the sacraments. Her faith inspired her with a thousand means of awakening in souls the love of Jesus in the most Blessed Sacrament. When persons visited her, she rarely let them go without showing them the chapel, and embracing the opportunity of saying a few words on the Real Presence. She loved to instil into the minds of the country-women that the church in no way resembled the ordinary home.

"The church-bell," she would say, "breaks forth high above your cottages and is heard at a great distance. When in the midst of your lands and vineyards, as the sound of the bell reaches you, let it remind you that Jesus is there ready to hear, enlighten, and bless you, his children."

Whenever they confided their troubles to her, after having listened attentively, and given them the advice she deemed proper, she added: "I do not know how to comfort you. Go awhile to the church, and tell our Lord what you have told me. He knows all, but he wishes you to confide in Him; afterwards say an 'Our Father' and 'Hail, Mary,' and be assured you will receive more strength and consolation than I can even picture to you."

She experienced so great grief on seeing our Lord in the Blessed Sacrament for hours and hours without adorers, that she could not even speak on the subject without manifesting emotion. "It would seem," she often said, "that we are blind and insensible, to remain poor and afflicted when all the bountiful treasures of divine love are at our disposal." This admirable confidence in God, which was the foundation of all the virtues of Mother St. Joseph, was not fully developed in her soul without rude combats. Sometimes the thought of what she had suffered at Belley and at Gap brought discouragement and disquietude for the future. These sentiments show themselves in a letter which she wrote in the month of January to Father Depery. After having acquainted him with their situation at Barsac, she added:

"God knows what will be the result of all this suffering. But with the bitter remembrance of the inconstancy and injustice of men, even of holy men, it is surprising that I have any desire to commence anew, and I oftentimes ask God to let me die before I undertake any new enterprises. However, God's will is my will, and I fully forgive those who have injured me."

At other times it seemed to her that her conduct was temerity itself—that she had neither material resources, nor the understanding necessary to found a work such as she was undertaking. Her past life itself seemed a series of illusions. She suffered interior torture and experienced a lively desire to abandon everything.

One evening, being more sorrowful than usual, she fell asleep while meditating on the words of Gamaliel to the Jews: "For if this work be of men, it will come to naught; but if it be of God, you cannot overthrow it, lest perhaps you be found even to fight against God." In her sleep she saw a magnificent tree entirely covered with blossoms. As she was admiring it, she perceived Father Pichat near her, and she said to him, with her old confidence: "Father, you know me better than I know myself. Tell me, I pray you, in what state you find my soul."

"Daughter," he replied, "your love for God is not disinterested. While persuading yourself that you seek only God, you seek yourself in many things. This tree is the figure of your soul."

Immediately the tree was stripped of its blossoms, which strewed the ground.

The priest added: "You put forth many blossoms, but few of them bring fruit to maturity."

At these words the vision vanished, and Mother St. Joseph awoke calmer than usual, and firmly resolved to put aside all natural feelings, and pursue the work Providence assigned her.

The most necessary part of the work was the organization of a novitiate. From the beginning a great number of young girls of Barcas and vicinity presented themselves to be received; Mother St. Joseph allowed them entrance, and on examining their dispositions, the motives which actuated them, and their former habits of life, soon found that many of them were attracted by love of novelty. A want of religious instruction, levity of character, a great fondness for dress, were among the obstacles to a religious vocation. One only, Désire Destanque, of whom we have elsewhere spoken, was received as postulant on the 16th of February.

The good Mother took special care to form this soul, which, though well disposed to advance in perfection, was completely ignorant of the requirements of a religious house. Great pains were requisite to teach her to pray in a reverent tone, to incline her head at the *Gloria Patri*, and to conform with all the other formalities of custom; but no details seemed unimportant to Mother St. Joseph when the honor of God was concerned. She exhorted her to always keep herself in unison with her angel guardian, and unite with him and all the angels in their adoration of the august Trinity. She kept the postulant with herself as much as possible, and, while performing the various household duties with her, would require an account of her inmost thoughts. She would ask: "Of what are you thinking, child?"

"Nothing, mother."

"It is necessary for you to keep your mind occupied. Think of the Infant Jesus and of the Blessed Virgin, who at their home in Nazareth did what we are doing now. What were your thoughts during meditation?"

"A few were of God; the rest of my family."

"In your next meditation you must begin by saying to God: 'My God, I want to think of Thee alone during this half hour.'"

"O mother! I do wish to think of Him, but I can't."

"You can, my child; use these means. To-day you will perform three acts of mortification for letting your thoughts wander during meditation; and while at your work, instead of allowing your mind to dwell on every object presented to your imagination, you will revert to the subject of your spiritual reading, to the life and passion of our Lord, or the lives of the saints. Thus you will accustom your mind to keep subservient to your will. Before the end of the year you will have a relish for prayer and spiritual exercises; the time spent therein will be too short, and you will become a good religious, mild, amiable, and even gracious, without your knowing it."

"Mother, I can never reach that point."

"Certainly you will, my child, if you labor with perseverance and act with simplicity. You are learning a profession, and must make rapid progress when your teacher has no other pupil but yourself. You must, however, make good use of your time, for soon others will come in whom you must assist in teaching."

Several postulants presented themselves, but want of room prevented their admission. One, however, who was recommended by the vicar-general, was received. Mother St. Joseph asked for means to raise the roof and furnish the garret for dormitory purposes; but the archbishop refused, fearing that the number of religious would increase too rapidly. Mother St. Joseph was then obliged to use the class-room for a dormitory at night, and remove the beds from it every morning. This arrangement enabled her to receive six postulants.

The proper instruction of these young girls was attended with great difficulty, on account of the numerous duties which engaged the time of the Sisters. Fortunately, Father Montceni came in July to spend the vacation with Father Lacoste, and he spent the greater part of the time teaching the various sciences to the postulants.

In August, matters being better organized, the superior asked for a canonical examination, which was made by Father Chanie, superior of the Marianites at Verdelais, and on the 25th of the month the archbishop gave the habit to the two oldest postulants. The ceremony took place in the parish church, which was found too small to contain the number who came to witness the event. His grace was accompanied by a great many clergy and several laics of distinction. The moving eloquence of the prelate and the ceremonies, witnessed for the first time by the assembly, rendered the day memorable at Barsac.

His grace visited the convent, and was welcomed with heart-felt joy by the community.

CHAPTER XXXIII.

SHE RENEWS A REQUEST TO ESTABLISH A NOVITIATE AT BORDEAUX.

THE old parochial residence occupied by the Sisters was found too small, and the persevering foundress requested the archbishop to allow her to establish the congregation at Bordeaux. It seemed to her that the work would progress better and be established more firmly in the episcopal city, under the immediate supervision of the ecclesiastical superior. In a visit which she paid to the archbishop in September, she earnestly urged her project. The wise prelate asked for time to reflect upon the proposition, and some days afterwards sent his decision. He wrote: "No one knows better than yourself that important projects cannot be accomplished in a day.

Your coming into my diocese appeared to me truly providential, and the good you have already done at Barsac proves to me that God wishes you here." He thought of establishing the Sisters at Verdelais, but the project met with too many obstacles. He could not think of taking the Sisters to Bordeaux when about to organize religious houses at three other places—Bazas, Sauve, and Verdelais. "I believe," he added, "God wishes you to open your novitiate at Barsac in reward for the heroic self-sacrifice of the priest there, and for the zeal of the good people who have assisted you." He advised her to procure a large house surrounded by ample grounds, formerly used by the Marianite Brothers. He ceded to Mother St. Joseph the revenue of the property in St. Aubin belonging to the diocese, and situated near St. Médard. This property consisted of about two acres, which had been given to the Trappist Brothers, and which had been used by them for some time. They had been forced to leave the place on account of the decease of several of their members, whose places could not be filled, and also on account of the disorders consequent on the revolution of 1830.

Mother St. Joseph was exceedingly moved at the kindness shown in the letter.; and, notwithstanding her great repugnance to establishing a novitiate at Barsac, she carefully followed the instructions of the prelate. The specified house was purchased October 18, 1841, and on the 28th the Sisters took possession. In November following the archbishop appointed Father la Tour, his vicar-general, superior of the congregation; and on the 30th of December his grace visited the new establishment, and offered the holy sacrifice of the Mass in the little chapel. In a touching address he exhorted the novices and postulants to make good use of the graces which God had conferred on them, and, under the wise direction of Mother St. Joseph, to lead lives truly fervent, as worthy models for those who would come after them, and thus form a solid foundation for their religious edifice.

Postulants came from different parts of France; ecclesiastics, religious, even laics, interested themselves in swelling the number. The good Mother was delighted at the progress of her work, and applied herself with renewed zeal to form her daughters to the practice of religious virtues.

All were obliged to rise at the first sound of the bell, and to be in the chapel at twenty minutes after five A.M. The postulants were surprised on entering the chapel to find Mother St. Joseph prostrate at the foot of the altar. At recreation she was asked how she dressed so quickly, and she answered: "I dress as quickly as possible, for I long to be near Jesus in the Blessed Sacrament, to thank Him for preserving me during the night, and promise to employ the day His love has granted me in loving Him with all my heart, and thus merit to be one day united to Him for all eternity."

After this, each member of the community tried to be first in the chapel. After morning prayers, the Mother would often make the meditation in a loud voice, in order to teach the novices to put in practice the method she taught them.

During the day she would require them to give an account of the thoughts and impressions they experienced during meditation, and she pointed out to them a thousand means to accustom them to converse with God.

Silence was one of the practices most recommended. "Our Lord," said she, "loves to speak to our hearts, but we must give Him our whole attention. Should you make a disturbance while I am talking, you would certainly show great disrespect thereby. How great forgetfulness, then, not to listen to the voice of Jesus in our hearts. A novice or religious who, during silence, speaks without necessity, or disturbs the quiet of the house in opening or closing doors, walking heavily, or in any other way, not only interrupts the voice of God, who speaks to her heart, but also disturbs the recollection of her companions, and places obstacles to their progress in the spiritual life." She imposed a severe penance for the infraction of the rule of silence in the dormitory or refectory. Her injunctions on this point were well observed, and at certain times the silence which pervaded the house was so profound as almost to make one believe it was uninhabited.

She attached great importance to the recitation of the Office. The pastor at Barsac came several times a week to teach the novices to read and pronounce the Latin. Mother St. Joseph demanded that every syllable be articulated distinctly, and that all the ceremonies be performed with gravity and recollection. "The religious," she said, "prays not alone in her own name when she recites the Office; she prays in union with the whole church and for the whole universe. She commits an injustice, then, if she does not acquit herself of that great duty in a suitable manner."

The most humble employments particularly attracted her attention. She herself superintended the household work. All the Sisters, the postulants, and the novices were employed in the different duties of the house, besides giving daily attention to the cultivation of their large garden.

The aim of all her efforts was to inspire the novices with an ardent zeal for the salvation of souls. "You are here," she said, "to become apostles."

The happy results of so many efforts were pleasingly apparent to the archbishop when, on the morning of the 25th of August, he gave the habit to nine postulants and received the vows of the first two professed. The ceremony took place in the church at Barsac in presence of a great concourse of people. The prelate, surprised at the great progress of the work and the evident assurance of its future success, resolved to transfer the novitiate to Bordeaux as soon as circumstances would permit. Providence, who ever mingles with our joys the holy perfume of grief and sacrifice, had just subjected Mother St. Joseph to a great trial in the severe illness of Sister Immaculate Conception. In the extremity of danger in which the Sister was the Mother had recourse to the Blessed Virgin with a lively faith, and she made a vow to take the sick Sister to Our Lady of Talence if she recovered. She had heard of this pilgrimage, situated near Bordeaux, and she felt herself impelled to invoke our Blessed

Lady under that title. Her prayer was heard, and soon after she went to Talence with the Sister to accomplish her vow. The church at the pilgrimage was then in course of erection. A sort of cabin made of boards contained, for the time being, the statue of the Blessed Virgin. Mother St. Joseph was extremely touched at the sight of the statue of Our Lady of Sorrows. The simplicity of the place, the recollection of the assistants, the fervor of the priests who in turn celebrated the Holy Sacrifice on the poor altar, the number of votive offerings, the favor she had just obtained, all combined to increase her emotion. From that day forward there existed an intimate and mysterious link binding her mind and soul to Talence, the effects of which will be seen later.

CHAPTER XXXIV.

GENEROSITY OF THE ARCHBISHOP.

THE archbishop, notwithstanding the care and expense attendant on the great work about to be organized, ceased not to confer marks of benevolence on the new congregation. In April, 1842, he gave the revenue of the old seminary of Moulere, near Cardan—a property he had purchased to put an end to several difficulties. Mother St. Joseph, in thanking him, told him she had just received seven postulants. A little later the generous prelate formed the resolution to contribute personally to the foundation of the particular houses which should afterwards be established.

The development of the novitiate, and the great interest the archbishop manifested in it, caused the people of Barsac to suspect that a removal to Bordeaux was contemplated. This suspicion was evinced in letters from the mayor and other leading citizens of Barsac to the archbishop. The people of Barsac felt that to take away Mother St. Joseph would be to visit them with an affliction which they had not deserved. "Our only fault," said they, "is to have understood the first day what others perceived only after years—the value of Mother St. Joseph. Barsac is but two hours' journey from Bordeaux, and we have ground enough to build a large convent, the plan of which is already drawn. Twenty thousand francs will be sufficient for the work; daily distributions can be made to the needy and distressed; and, later, the house can be enlarged for the accommodation of five hundred religious. At Bordeaux the cost of erection of a convent, and also the maintenance of the Sisters, will be double what it is here; besides, the prospect of a hospital at Barsac must die out with the departure of Mother St. Joseph from among us."

These reasonings and pleadings were

overruled, in the mind of the archbishop, by the consideration of greater advantages resulting from the removal of the novitiate to Bordeaux. Late in 1842 measures were taken to purchase a property suitable for the purpose, and Mother St. Joseph selected the Champs Elysées, which had been used as a pleasure-ground for some years, and was then offered her by the curé of St. Bruno. The idea of having God praised and honored where he had previously been offended pleased both the curé and Mother St. Joseph; but the archbishop disapproved of their plans, saying that the clergy and people of Bordeaux would object to the location. Many other projects were entered into and discarded, until finally the archbishop became discouraged, and was about to abandon the intention of establishing them in the place. Not so with Mother St. Joseph. Opposition and disappointment served but to awaken all the latent energy in her nature, and determined her to succeed. The archbishop and vicar-general urged her to make a foundation at St. Seurin de Cadourne. The curé of that place, Father Bureau, wrote to her September 23, 1842: "I await your visit to make final arrangements for the coming of the Sisters. If I cannot find a suitable house, I will give my own rather than forego the advantages of a school for the children. I beg of you do not refuse my application." The good Mother could not refuse, and on the 3d of October following she installed three Sisters at St. Seurin. She placed Sister St. Paul in charge as superior, confident that the experience and virtues of this religious would make the first foundation a secure one. It was no small sacrifice to the community at Barsac that the example of obedience and fervor of Sister St. Paul was lost to the younger members. A letter from Sister St. Paul to Rev. Mother St. Benedict, dated November 8, 1842, shows that the community at Barsac at this time numbered twenty-six religious, as many professed as novices, and this number was on the point of being increased by four. In answer to this letter Mother St. Benedict expressed her pleasure at the prosperity of the new foundation: "I have long desired to hear from you and your dear Mother, whom I do not forget, though she seems to have become oblivious of me. Assure her of my love, and say to her I am often with her before the Tabernacle, and pray there that God may ever bless her and all her undertakings." She goes on to give an account of the community of Champagne, and says: "The good spirit you implanted there still lives in the Sisters; when a structure has a good foundation, it is always solid and lasting."

Father Colletta, of Oyonnax, near Nantua, wrote to Mother St. Joseph: "You embarrass me in requiring me to give you my opinion of yourself and community, and I can only answer in your own words: 'The desire of the just shall not perish.' Have the will to please God in all things, and rest in perfect security." The pious curé insisted on the importance of teaching the young postulants the necessity of absolute sincerity in confession, and advised her to be particular in giving instructions on this point. This advice was faithfully followed by her. She had a particular gift of discernment of hearts, and would often induce those under her charge to tell her their most hidden thoughts. One day a postulant who had just finished her general confession, and appeared to be animated with the best of sentiments, asked permission to receive Holy Communion. The Mother looked at her, and, instead of granting the permission, took her aside, and, notwithstanding the manifest desire of the young girl to evade her questions, forced her to acknowledge that she had voluntarily concealed a grievous sin in her confession. Then, instead of annoying her with reproaches, she tried to strengthen her by exhortations and encouragements, and sent her back to the confessional. She returned to the Mother after a short time, and told her that now her conscience was at rest, that she had confessed all; but Mother St. Joseph reproved her, saying: "Do you imagine you can deceive God, as you are trying to deceive me?" She imposed a penance on her, advised her to earnestly and humbly pray God to free her from the dumb devil that held possession of her soul, and promised to unite with her in praying for this intention. In a few days their petition was granted, and the peace of a good conscience was restored to the postulant, and her gratitude to God was shown in her perfect conversion. Often the superior would say to the curé of Barsac: "Father, I will send a certain Sister again to confession to you; please question her on certain matters." She did all in her power to allow full liberty of conscience to the Sisters, and always called in any confessor the Sisters might wish for; and this she did when the first wish to that effect was expressed. Her gift of reading hearts was shown in the admission of postulants. One day two young girls visited her to make arrangements to enter the novitiate the following year. Both were received with her usual courtesy, but, after exchanging words with one of them, she took the other aside and instructed her in the measures to be taken and preparation to be made for entrance. Moreover, she showed confidence, affection, and interest in her while she scarcely noticed the other. At the appointed time only the last-mentioned entered; and some time later on, speaking of the difference in the reception of both, Mother St. Joseph explained by saying that from the first she saw that God had called both to the religious life, but the one towards whom she manifested so great confidence was exposed to many dangers of losing her vocation, while the other had no obstacles whatever to retard her in her pious intention. And her fears were verified in the case of the girl; for she remained deaf to the call of God, and established herself in the world. She never allowed a young girl who sought admission to leave her without mortifying her self-love, or humbling a Sister in her presence; and from the impression made on the postulant and her reception of the trial, she judged her simplicity of heart and spirit of docility. As subjects were generally required to wait some time after application for entrance, she advised them always to make good use of the interval to learn the practice of humility, obedience, and self-denial—virtues which would be required of them during their whole lives. She loved generous souls and those having strong wills, and she taught them from their very entrance to direct those qualities in the way that would be productive of most good. "When we renounce the world and ourselves to follow

Jesus Christ," said she, "we give Him nothing; it is He who gives us a proof of His infinite love and kindness in calling us to the religious life, as we thus become His spouses. However, He regards our severances of all ties as great sacrifices, and will reward us accordingly. 'And every one that hath left house, or brethren, or sisters, or father, or mother, or wife, or children, or lands, for my name's sake, shall receive a hundred-fold, and shall possess life everlasting.'"

The early days of 1843 were rendered memorable by a terrible inundation. The Garonne overflowed its usual bounds and covered the land. The bourg of Barsac suffered particularly, being submerged during eight days. Steamboats navigated the streets of the city, and the water rose to the ground-floor of the convent. The Sisters sought refuge in the upper story, and spent a week in great anxiety. The novices and young Sisters were greatly terrified; for the waves dashed against the walls of the house with a force that threatened to crumble it in ruins. Mother St. Joseph, whose confidence in God was unbounded, reanimated the courage of the despondent by her calm and even good-humor. After having taken all necessary precautions, she obtained a boat, and, with the curé of Barsac and a Sister, visited others who suffered from the effects of the flood, and took whatever she could obtain for their relief. The devastation produced by the inundation caused great misery in the country for several months after the waters had subsided. Both the charitable curé, M. Labonne, and the Sisters deprived themselves of everything to supply the wants of the distressed. Towards the end of February the letter-carrier brought a letter directed to Mother St. Joseph, and having eighty centimes due as postage. Not having wherewith to redeem the letter, the carrier was allowed to go; but, on a moment's reflection, she sent a Sister to tell the carrier that she would pay postage the following day if he left the letter. The Sister obeyed, but doubted the possibility of the postage being paid as promised. What was her surprise, on seeing the letter opened, to find it contained an order for three hundred francs. A few days afterwards the archbishop sent two hundred francs, and a religious person, whose name was not given, sent two hundred more. Mother St. Joseph, transported with joy and gratitude, repeated the words of Scripture: "Seek first the kingdom of God and His justice, and all things else shall be added unto you." "See, my children," she said, "the goodness of God to us. Be always humble and of no account in your own eyes, conform your will to that of God, and His providence will ever watch over you. He knows the wants of even the most obscure among His children."

The great fatigue Mother St. Joseph underwent during the time of the inundation impaired her health so as to render her unable to attend to her duties. For a time she was threatened with amaurosis; and while this disease of the eyes was being treated, inflammation of the lungs set in. While she was convalescing the church at Barsac took fire, and the fright caused by the event brought on a relapse. However, she recovered sufficiently to sit in a chair during the early part of Holy Week. On Holy Thursday, the 13th of April, she made her hour of adoration before the most Blessed Sacrament, notwithstanding the urgent pleadings of the Sisters to the contrary. She commenced the pious exercise at eleven o'clock, and prayed until midnight, in union with Jesus in the Garden of Olives. Her heart was so filled with grief at the consideration of the sadness that oppressed the heart of Jesus when he uttered the words, "My soul is sorrowful unto death," that she shed tears constantly. The Sisters were deeply moved at her emotion, and united their prayers with hers. At midnight she ceased praying, and remained motionless until about two o'clock, when the Sisters persuaded her to retire to rest, though all the time her mind was absorbed with the sorrows of Jesus. The Sisters remarked afterwards that they then for the first time understood the hour of adoration.

On the 17th of May the archbishop officiated at a reception; and again during the same year, on August 23, received the profession of several novices and gave the habit to a number of postulants. After the ceremony his grace visited Father Labonne, who was ill at the time, suffering from the effects of privations and exposure during the inundation. The archbishop had tendered the good priest all the relief in his power, but the kindness and care came too late to arrest the hand of death. In this last visit he proposed removing him to the episcopal residence. The priest thanked him, with assurances of sincerest gratitude, for all he had done for him, and also for sending Mother St. Joseph to Barsac. He said he regretted life only because he had hoped to devote it entirely to the good of the new congregation. He lingered a few days after this, and died on the morning of the 4th of September, in sentiments of lively faith and most tender piety. The day preceding his death he told Mother St. Joseph that he would not live until morning. She was greatly afflicted at the death of her pastor, but sought consolation in prayer and in the hope of his happiness. She was consoled, too, in the thought that he would be spared the sorrow of seeing the novitiate removed to Bordeaux—an event to which she looked forward, notwithstanding all appearances to the contrary.

CHAPTER XXXV.

PURCHASE OF A CONVENT AT BORDEAUX.

EFFORTS were made by different interested parties at Bordeaux to purchase a house suitable for the establishment of the Sisters, but without success, until one day Mother St. Joseph met two women who expressed a desire to have an interview with her. They told her that they had resided some years with the community of Marie Thérèse, where Mother St. Joseph lodged on her arrival at Bordeaux, and they had left it a short time previous to establish a boarding and day school under their own direction. They had purchased a house situated near Aquitaine, and furnished it for the purpose. At this time they had a large number of scholars in attendance, but could not save sufficient means to make payments on their purchase. They offered to place the house, furniture, and pupils at the disposal of Mother St. Joseph, and they expressed a desire to place themselves under her direction, with the view of becoming religious. She regarded this opportunity as an intervention of divine Providence; but, not wishing to act hastily in the matter, she asked the women to reflect on their offer and pray that the will of God might be accomplished. Nevertheless, she returned to Barsac, convinced that steps would soon be taken to found a house at Bordeaux, where the congregation could increase in proportion to the wants of the diocese.

Two new foundations were made during this interval—one at Pauillac and another at Sauterne, the latter of which was maintained but a short time for want of Sisters. Mother St. Joseph never established a house where the parish could not support three Sisters, as less than this number could not live in the practice of religious obedience, humility, and charity. The community at Pauillac flourished under the patronage of the city officers, and they established an orphan asylum in connection with the day-schools.

On the 20th of September Mother St. Joseph and Sister Immaculate Conception went to Gap, with the approbation of the archbishop, to put the affairs of the community there in order. She relinquished all her rights to the property of the congregation at Gap, with the exception of five thousand francs, which she wished to retain for the benefit of the future novitiate at Bordeaux. In returning she stopped at Lyons, and left Sister Immaculate Conception there to make purchases while she went to visit the venerable curé of Ars, with whom she was intimately united in prayers during many years. She longed to converse with him on the state of her soul, and to consult him on the future of her work. M. Viannay was pleased to see her, and he acquainted her with his trouble, similar to her own in the transfer of the house of Providence. He told her to rely entirely on the goodness and bounty of God, and assured her that if it were necessary to the success of the religious congregation at Bordeaux to perform miracles,

God would perform them in her favor. Mary Jane Chanay, a cousin to Mother St. Joseph, and who resided with the pious curé, told her of the many conversions and prodigies which daily took place at Ars, so that the good Mother returned to Lyons, her soul deeply moved at what she had seen and heard, and filled with more ardor and generosity than ever to work the great work of God.

She returned to Barsac the 14th of October, and after the general retreat she went to Bordeaux to make final arrangements for the purchase of the house previously mentioned. The contract was drawn up in presence of a notary, November 16, 1843. Two days afterwards she heard of the death of Mother St. Benedict, superior-general of Bourg, whose heart was for years united to hers by those strong ties that only Christian charity can bind. Her grief was softened by the remembrance of the virtues of her much-regretted friend. In writing to Bishop Devie she spoke of the great worth of the deceased. Sister St. Claude was appointed to succeed her as superior. This religious was received by Mother St. Joseph at Belley, and made her profession at Bourg. While the chapter Sisters were assembled to decide upon her admission to vows, some one among them said that she would one day be superior of the congregation. Mother St. Joseph communicated this to the bishop. He wrote to her saying that when he received her letter Sister St. Claude had already been place in charge, to the general satisfaction of the Sisters and the good of the congregation. He congratulated Mother St. Joseph on the progress of her great work, and, after speaking of the Sisters of Gap, says: "You tell me I ought to know your reason for not writing to me. I really see no cause for silence, unless it be that we are too far distant for me to be of any service to you; and, perhaps, because I somewhat wounded your feelings by the recommendations I gave you in my last letter. I have confidence, however, that, after a little reflection before God, you will fully understand that all I said was prompted by a desire that you may become more humble and more faithful to God's grace. This is the language I have always used with you, and I believe such to be most conformable to your wants. The gift of prophecy gives us no merit before God, whereas humility is always necessary and meritorious."

Another letter bearing the signature of Bishop Devie, dated January, 1844, refers to the impropriety of asking the authorization of the government for the foundation at Bordeaux. He says: "The present time is unfavorable; for the Sisters at Gap have just been refused the privilege. Better be satisfied with the regulations of Bourg." He then writes in a postscript: "Insisting on humility is a new proof of the supernatural interest I take in a person who needs to be brought occasionally to the cradle of the One who descended so low, certainly not to teach us to become great and popular." These lines are copied to show the friendly relations existing between these two souls, beautiful in virtue, and separated by distance and rank.

As soon as the Sisters were given possession of the house at Bordeaux, it became known at Barsac that the novitiate was to be removed. A general outburst of grief followed the announcement. Mother St. Joseph sought to satisfy the people by assuring them that a large establishment would always be maintained there, and that she herself would remain there for some months.

On the 9th of January, 1844, she sent Sisters St. Paul and Mary and a novice to take possession of the house at Bordeaux and direct the day-school. The old proprietors were to continue in charge of the academy until the arrival of Mother St. Joseph.

On the 19th of March the bishop officiated at the last profession made at Barsac. He spoke of zeal for the salvation of souls, and of the great necessity for numerous religious establishments to aid him in the cultivation of the vast field God had entrusted to his care.

Immediately after this ceremony, Mother St. Joseph received news from Sister St. Paul to the effect that the women from whom the house at Bordeaux was purchased had deceived her in their pretence of becoming religious, and that they were using undue influence on the novice, who, she feared, would leave the community and join them. This letter caused her great sadness, but, as consolation always accompanies or follows grief, she received a communication from Bishop Devie, wherein he says: "I learn with no small pleasure that the good God is blessing your labors. I exhort you to continue them with confidence and zeal, but above all with humility; for this last virtue is the foundation of the spiritual edifice. Keep yourself closely united to God in heart and in soul, avoid friendships that are too human, and seek in everything God's greater glory." He sent with this letter thirty copies of his works for the use of the Sisters.

Mother St. Joseph heard of the nomination of her tried and faithful friend, Father Depery, to the see of Gap. She writes: "My heart is filled with joy, and I experience too great satisfaction. I congratulate you, dear father, now bishop; but, alas! I fear that at Gap as well as everywhere else crosses await you."

Bishop Depery responded the 29th of May, and says: "My dear Sister, I am caught in a snare. On my arrival at Paris I heard for the first time the news of my appointment. I was sent there to solicit funds for the cathedral, and though all France knew of the nomination, I was ignorant of it. I cannot describe my feelings in the sight of my Calvary better than by telling you I endured as much sorrow as is possible for a human heart to endure and live. If you were near me, good Sister, you could be my providence in this emergency. Pray then, and have others pray for me. According to my promise, I will leave my beautiful Lechaud to the Sisters of St Joseph."

This letter was forwarded to Mother St. Joseph at Bordeaux, where she had been called on account of the serious illness of Sister St. Mary. Her stay in the city gave her an opportunity of seeing the true condition of affairs. The women who made the sale of the house and furniture had already rented a building in the neighborhood, furnished it, and intended to take the silver plate and some other articles that belonged by agreement to Mother St. Joseph. This latter project was prevented. The pupils were taught to revolt against the authority of the Sisters, and, as soon as opportunity presented itself, they rebelled. Mother St. Joseph immediately determined what course to pursue. She closed the boarding-school, dismissed all the pupils in attendance, except four, which she sent to Barsac, and continued the day-school. The two women left on July 4, and circulated almost incredible calumnies relative to the Sisters, who were strangers in Bordeaux. "The Sisters," they said, "gained the confidence of honorable persons by their deceitful promises, and wished to obtain means under false pretences." These women even went so far as to have published pamphlets, containing accusations most injurious to the Sisters, distributed through the city; and, as usually happens, these were exaggerated through every medium. A lawsuit was threatened against Mother St. Joseph, and the trouble was ended by an arbitration, which completely justified the Sisters. During all this time Mother St. Joseph was not in the least disturbed; for she knew by experience that the works most conducive to God's glory meet with most opposition. She was, moreover, upheld by the counsel of the archbishop, and she looked upon the trial as a proof of the good to be in time accomplished by means of the establishment at Bordeaux. On leaving the house of the judge, who decided in her favor, she remarked to the Sister who accompanied her: "After all, these women meant no harm, but God saw this trial necessary for me."

CHAPTER XXXVI.

NOVITIATE AT BORDEAUX.

THE novitiate was transferred to Bordeaux June 13, 1844. On the 20th of the same month Mother St. Joseph received a visit from her old benefactor, M. Pasquier. In order to lead a life more in conformity with the maxims of the Gospel, he had disposed of all his wealth at Lyons, and proposed to rebuild the Chartreuse of Montrieux, situated a short distance from Hyères. But before accomplishing this purpose he wished to spend a few months at Bordeaux, where he could receive spiritual direction from Mother St. Joseph, and render her temporal aid in the organization of her work. He brought her a present of a magnificent crucifix wrought in ivory.

On the 16th of July the first profession took place at Bordeaux. Rev. Father Borredon, curé of Juillac, presided at the request of the archbishop. This venerable priest met Mother St. Joseph for the first time in a coach on her way to Gap, and he was so prepossessed in her favor by her conversation and charity that he wished to become acquainted with her. He gladly complied with the request of his grace, and after his return to Juillac he wrote to Mother St. Joseph: "I gladly embraced the opportunity of going to Bordeaux; for I wished to satisfy myself of your disinterested zeal and charity, which were but imperfectly known to me. I shall labor with you in spirit and in prayer, and I am desirous that you be known and appreciated by my people, who will hardly be convinced of your heroic self-sacrifice in behalf of others. I was more than pleased with the piety and admirable charity of your community, and shall always retain the impression made among my most agreeable remembrances." This father was ever after a most zealous patron of the congregation.

The house was indeed a model religious institution, and the superior gave a perfect example of all the virtues of a religious. She lived in the midst of her Sisters as one of them, assisted at all the exercises and gave special attention to the manner in which the Sisters spent their recreations. She established her dwelling in the community-room, and held private conferences with the Sisters in an adjoining apartment, that she might vigilantly guard all under her care. She would say: "The edifice is but commenced; in order to have it well built, its material and construction must be well selected and directed."

She inculcated a love of industry and economy, and the spirit of penance and charity. "My children," she would say, "do not lose a moment of time, and watch over everything confided to your care as you would over a great treasure. It requires but little to have each of us lose or waste the value of two cents a day, either in time or goods; and this loss would amount on the whole to six francs a day, which could be disposed of for the relief of the poor. Compute the sum saved in a month, and see how many poor families you could make happy and comfortable without taking from the community. Order, economy, and labor—these three words contain the secret of managing a house well, and being enabled to assist the poor." By seeing that these qualities were practised in all employments, she cultivated a love for them among the Sisters. Although she was of a generous disposition, she could not bear to see an article of even the smallest value wasted without admonishing the author for the want of poverty, and assuring her that negligence in small things is contrary to its spirit.

One day she heard of a family in the neighborhood in distress, and, being unable to pay their debts, a creditor was about to sell the small remnant of their furniture. She agreed with the Sisters to add to their ordinary savings for the poor other privations for a time, until a sufficient sum for the relief of the distressed family could be collected. She was told that, if the paid the creditor in question, others would seize upon the furniture, and that it would be impossible for her to satisfy all. Accordingly, she went to the place of sale, herself bought the furniture, and returned it to the family for their use, with the understanding that she retained ownership. She would not listen to the expressions of thanks and gratitude from the poor family, but left their cabin to procure steady and profitable employment for them.

Among the extra labors undertaken by the Sisters, the principal was the raising of silk-worms, and from the profits of this alone Mother St. Joseph paid the expenses of two young men who entered the novitiate of the Christian Brothers at Caluire, near Lyons. By her advice several persons engaged in the cultivation of mulberry-trees, and even the archbishop had his country residence surrounded by them. The good Mother succeeded so well in raising them, and contributed so much to the progress of industry in the Gironde, that the Industrial Society awarded her a prize in September, 1844.

The first reception and profession at Bordeaux took place on the 29th of September. Mother St. Joseph wished the ceremony to take place, if possible, on the

Feast of St. Michael every year, on account of her great confidence in the powerful protection of that celestial prince. After the ceremony, at which his grace officiated, he advised two new foundations—Lormont and Bazas.

The first was greatly desired by the zealous pastor, Father Joly, but some of the parishioners were opposed to it on account of a school, conducted by laics, which was already established there. Mother St. Joseph went with three Sisters to open a house in the parish, and she paid little or no attention to the difficulties predicted for them.

She told the Sisters they would surmount all difficulties by prudence, the spirit of sacrifice, and confidence in God, and she warned them against intercourse with any one except the pupils confided to their care. She advised them to always speak in favor of the secular teachers, even though the latter were unfriendly towards them; "for," she said, "persons are everywhere found who are but too willing to sow dissension and carry reports." The Sisters were faithful to her instructions;

their school prospered, and in a short time they were called upon to found an orphan asylum, which soon gave refuge to one hundred children. Eighteen years afterwards some one observed to Father Joly that the foundation at Lormont did not succeed well, on account of the secular school in the place. But he assured the person that it was a perfect success; that not only did the Sisters fulfil all the duties expected from them, but the secular teachers modelled their system of instruction as much as possible after the example of the Sisters, and that the children under their care were taught the catechism, proper behavior in the church, and decorum in the streets. Four Sisters were sent to the college at Bazas to take charge of the infirmary and the wardrobe of the students. The good Mother advised prudence and reserve on the part of the Sisters, and told them that they should not imagine their duties less meritorious than those of Sisters employed in the instruction of youth; for in acquitting themselves of the work assigned them they would contribute to the prosperity of an institution devoted to the education of pious and learned ecclesiastics. She gave them the Blessed Virgin and the Infant Jesus in the house at Nazareth for their models, and reminded them that there is more merit in sweeping an apartment through obedience than in doing great works by one's own will.

Towards the end of this year Mother St. Joseph heard, through Father Colletta, of the trouble occasioned Bishop Devie by some of his clergy, who sent charges to the government against his administration. This news was a cause of great grief to her. She writes to Father Colletta: "Had I followed the impulses of my heart, I would have gone at once to comfort him and defend his cause; but, alas! what good could I do him?" She wrote to the bishop himself, and he answered her, January 10, 1845: "I am very grateful, my dear daughter, for the prayers you have said and the sympathy you show for me. We must expect these little miseries while we are in the world and while we have before our eyes the Crucified, who is our model. Moreover, the storm has caused more noise than injury." After having told her of the House of Providence, he gives his usual lesson of humility: "Be humble, very humble; speak less of yourself, of your acquaintance, of your family, and depend entirely on the goodness and mercy of God. I trust He will fill your heart with an abundance of spiritual consolation."

The affairs of the congregation required Mother St. Joseph some time after this to make a journey to Lyons and Belley. She left Bordeaux February 10, accompanied by Sister St. Paul, after having received the blessing of the archbishop. A heavy snow covered the ground, and rendered the roads through the mountain-passes very dangerous and difficult. Mother St. Joseph found occasion to practise charity towards the travellers, and particularly the guide, who was almost frozen. Her departure in the midst of winter for so long an absence and so dangerous a journey rendered her parting from the Sisters exceedingly painful. Nothing can show better the union of hearts between the good superior and her spiritual children than the simple and feeling letters exchanged by them. She writes, February 16: "I have but one desire, which is to have all my dear daughters with me; and hope bids me take courage, for in a few days my wish will be granted of seeing you once more. Take good care of yourselves, and do not weep for your Mother; for I assure you she does not weep for you. We must be reasonable and offer our separation as a sacrifice to our Lord in behalf of the souls in purgatory. Adieu. Do not be uneasy about us. Sister St. Paul and myself are well." And again, on the 8th of March, she writes: "Good-morning, my beloved daughters. I have just been praying the good God for you all. You believe this, my dear children; for you know your Mother loves you better than herself, and this is the reason your letters make her forget everything but the dear writers."

She reached Belley on the 24th of February, very early in the morning, and immediately paid an unexpected visit to her dear Providence. Her presence was the signal for universal joy. A simultaneous "Our Mother!" was heard, and young and old were beside themselves with delight. During the day she called on Bishop Devie, who expressed surprise at seeing her abroad in that severe season of the year, and also at the great improvement in her health and strength. He conversed with her several hours concerning her works at Bordeaux, and evinced great satisfaction at her success. He gave her most paternal recommendations for the preservation of her health. In the afternoon she again called on him and went to confession. Sister St. Paul had never before witnessed an interview between the bishop and Mother St. Joseph. She was aware of the circumstances under which she left Belley for Bordeaux, and more than once she heard of the severe reproaches given by the prelate to the Mother. She was, therefore, greatly surprised at the heartfelt welcome given her, and wondered how those two souls, so closely united in friendship, could cause each other so great suffering. The bishop took the Sister aside and enquired what she had heard at Chazay, while a boarder there, referring to the future departure of Mother St. Joseph for Bordeaux. She related the incident at recreation before given, and the bishop said: "Her life is a series of wonderful events." From that time until his death his letters to Mother St. Joseph were less severe, either on account of obtaining a truer knowledge of the interior state of his spiritual daughter, or because he felt satisfied with her advance in the path of humility. The only cloud that shadowed these two souls was their diversity of opinion concerning the transfer of title to the House of Providence at Belley, and this always remained. Before leaving the Diocese of Belley, Mother St. Joseph visited Bourg, where Mother St. Claude received her with marks of respect and affectionate regard; she also stopped at Chazay to settle some family affairs for Sister St. Paul. It was a great consolation to her to revisit the scenes of her first labors in the service of God, and where she had received so many favors. The inhabitants flocked to see the "little Sister St. Joseph of twenty years ago," and were surprised to meet an old religious on whose brow time and care had left their footprints.

Mother St. Joseph returned to Bordeaux

on the 22d of March, to the great joy of her dear daughters. A few days after her return, the archbishop sent her five hundred francs to be expended for the wants of the house, accompanied by a note: "I pray Mother St. Joseph to accept the enclosed as an offering made in thanksgiving for her safe return, and in gratitude for the dangers she escaped during her journey."

Sister Mary died the following May. Her health failed from the time of her arrival at Bordeaux. She was the daughter of a sea captain, and was one of the first who entered the novitiate at Barsac. Her religious life was marked by a strict observance of rule and great respect for her superiors. The day preceding her death, being in great pain, the priest who attended her gave her a relic of the Holy Cross, which she pressed to her lips with sensible devotion. One of the Sisters attempted to hang it around the neck of the patient, but she objected, to the surprise of all at her bedside. With great effort she gasped: "Ask Mother's permission for me to wear silver"; and on their complying she gratefully accepted the treasure.

This death was the first among the community at Bordeaux, and it gave a severe shock to Mother St. Joseph; for, notwithstanding her energy and great faith, she loved her daughters with a most tender love, and could never see one of them die without experiencing the deepest sorrow. After the retreat and the profession which took place at its close, three Sisters were sent to Moulis, a house established through the generosity of the Countess MacCarthy. An orphan asylum, named St. Eulalie, was also established at this time in the same parish at Bordeaux in which the novitiate was located.

CHAPTER XXXVII.

HER PRINCIPLES ON THE RECEPTION OF NO-
VICES—FATHER TAILLEFER NOMINATED SUPE-
RIOR.

IN 1841 Father de la Tour, vicar-general of the diocese, was appointed superior of the Sisters of St. Joseph, and from that time had labored zealously in the organization of the congregation; but his failing health, frequent absence, and other duties prevented him from giving the necessary attention to the Sisters. Consequently, in October, 1845, he asked and obtained a release from the appointment.

Mother St. Joseph prayed earnestly for several months that God would give them a superior according to His wish, and the one most calculated to promote the good of the congregation and His glory. Her prayer was answered in the nomination of Father Taillefer, canon of Bordeaux, and known throughout France as the founder of the Christian library. He took charge of the congregation in January, 1846, and from that time until his death, in 1868, the venerable ecclesiastic devoted all his time and attention to the interests of his charge.

A great number of young girls sought admission into the novitiate. After a first examination, the good Mother received those among them whom she thought were called to the religious life. "The novitiate,' she said, "is established for the purpose of knowing, examining, and correcting our faults and acquiring virtues." If, during their novitiate, the subjects did not make rapid progress in the spiritual life, she sent them home to their families without the slightest hesitancy. At least half the novices were rejected during their time of probation. Their dismissal gave frequent cause of displeasure to both the priests who recommended the subjects and their parents; but Mother St. Joseph was inflexible in her decisions. She made very little account of the dowry required from each postulant, and frequently refused to receive those who had large possessions, advising them to enter some order more in accordance with their mode of life than would be the poor Sisters of St. Joseph; while, on the contrary, she supplied poor girls having good dispositions with sufficient means to provide their outfit. She said: "There is a mint in heaven where is coined money to pay for the souls redeemed by the Precious Blood of Jesus, and called by Him to be His spouses. I much prefer receiving the dowry from God rather than from parents; He is goodness and generosity itself, and never counts what he gives." When she was admonished for receiving so many subjects without a dowry, she replied: "And would you, for the paltry sum of a few hundred francs, deprive souls of the happiness of consecrating themselves for ever to the service of God in the religious life, and thus deprive the Church of so many gems— the diocese of Sisters who will teach children the knowledge and love of Jesus Christ? Ah! no; I fear and love God too much to reject the souls which he has chosen."

The archbishop had been informed of her remissness in this respect, and he warned the new superior against it; but when the subject was mentioned to the Mother, she gave her reasons for the measure, and finished by saying: "Father, the archbishop may do his best; I am forced to cheat him in this particular." God visibly blessed her charity by causing the Sisters to endure sweetly and patiently all their privations, and always supplying their wants in a most providential manner. The archbishop himself frequently assisted them in emergencies.

In 1846 two new houses were established—one at Civræ and another at Salles. After accompanying the Sisters to each of these foundations, Mother St. Joseph made her first visitation of all the houses already founded in the diocese. The season being inclement and damp, she contracted a cold which settled on her lungs, and she returned to Bordeaux in a weak state of health. A constant cough prevented her from sleeping, and every day told on her declining strength. However, she attended all the community exercises, gave a spiritual conference every day, taught and explained the catechism for one hour, and made every effort to control the sickness by the energy of her will. One day, while assisting at an exercise, feeling faint, she called a Sister to help her to her room. Convinced that death was near, she told the Sister where to find the habit and veil in which she desired to be buried. The malady made alarming progress; two physicians were called in, and they gave little hope of her recovery. She kept her soul constantly united to God, and thanked the Sisters in attendance for their care of her. Fears for her death were entertained during the whole month of January, 1847. The archbishop visited her several times during her illness, and encouraged the Sisters to pray to God with confidence, and her recovery would be granted. Towards the end of the month they commenced a novena in honor of Our Lady of Talence. Nine Sisters walked to the church of Talence every day, prayed in the name of the community, and received Holy Communion there during the nine days. From the beginning of the novena a marked improvement was noticed in the condition of the dear patient, and on the Feast of the Purification the physicians pronounced her out of danger. All the Sisters went to the shrine at Talence on that day, and presented an ex-voto offering for their Mother's recovery.

On Friday, 26th of March, the Feast of Our Lady of Dolors, Mother St. Joseph was taken in a carriage to the shrine at Talence. Prostrating herself before the statue of Our Lady of Pity, she offered fervent thanksgiving for the favor accorded her, and begged Our Lady to bring about the foundation of a house of the order near Talence, that the Sisters might daily offer their petitions at her shrine. In returning to Bordeaux she walked the greater part of the way, and that day resumed the usual routine of exercises. At the request of her daughters she related what she experienced at the sanctuary, and told them she had promised an annual pilgrimage to be made there by the community on the Feast of Our Lady's Compassion.

The great energy of the good Mother made her forget that she was but convalescing, and she applied herself to the practices of mortification and prayer, and attended all the exercises of Holy Week. On Easter Sunday the fever returned and again placed her life in danger. The Sisters had recourse to a great servant of God, Father Bouet. This holy priest, remarkable for his great humility and austere manner of life, gave weekly conferences to the community, and shared their hopes, and fears, and troubles. He visited the patient, and exhorted her to offer a renewal of her intention to labor assiduously in the service of God and His poor, after the example of St. Martin, and left her presence to offer the Holy Sacrifice of the Mass for her intention. When he had finished his thanksgiving after Mass, he told the Sisters their Mother would recover, and said: "I am old and of little service to any one. I begged God to accept the sacrifice of my life and spare your Mother, and I feel that He is pleased with my petition. But she will be left among you for only a short time. Her soul is a tree laden with fruits ripe for heaven; at the first shock given it those fruits will be gathered into the celestial storehouse awaiting them." The following day Mother St. Joseph was entirely restored to health, and resumed her labors. The venerable father died a few months after, regretted by the Sisters and all who knew his worth. During Easter week one of the Sisters wrote to Bishop Devie, asking him to have a wax taper kept burning before the shrine of St. Anthelme for her intention. The bishop, with his natural severity, answered her: "I shall comply with your wish, and will also unite my prayers with yours for the recovery of your Mother; still, you must be well impressed with the truth that no one is necessary in this world to do the work of God, and that entire conformity to His divine will must be practised by all who sincerely love Him. Sacrifice is love." After the recovery of Mother St. Joseph, she made frequent visits to the shrine at Talence, and at each renewed her desire of establishing a house there. Want of means, however, deterred her from the undertaking, and she patiently awaited God's providence to bring about the desired event.

In the meantime Madame de Cercy, a lady who was not acquainted with Mother St. Joseph, experienced a desire to contribute towards the promotion of some charitable work. One day, after she had received Holy Communion in the chapel of Our Lady of Palais Gallien, she felt impelled to go to Talence. She immediately obeyed the inspiration, and, while praying before the statue, she noticed the ex-voto offering made by the Sisters of St. Joseph in gratitude for their Mother's recovery. The picture shed a ray of light into the soul of the pious lady, and she resolved to devote her means to the foundation of a school for the instruction of youth, and which should be given to a religious order. She communicated her design to the priest in charge of the parish, and he told her that a community of religious had already purchased property in the place, and would take charge of her projected foundation. She answered that she wished to have it under the direction of the Sisters who had placed the designated picture at the shrine.

The priest gave her Mother St. Joseph's address, and a letter wherein he urged the good Mother to accept the offer. She went to Talence shortly after receiving the letter, and property was purchased for twenty-five thousand francs, fourteen thousand of which were to be paid by Madame de Cercy, and the remainder by the community. The property was desirable on account of its location, being near the church, and situated on an elevation commanding a beautiful view and salubrious air. Mother St. Joseph destined it for the Sisters and novices for whom change of air and healthy location would be necessary; hence the difficulty of obtaining the eleven thousand francs and furnishing the house was no drawback to the purchase.

On the 1st of November, 1847, the Sisters took possession of their new home under the shadow of Mary's sanctuary, and the schools were opened on the same day.

Madame de Cercy was admitted into the convent as a boarder, and treated by the Sisters with all the attention and respect their gratitude inspired. But in time she conceived the idea of establishing a new congregation, and used her influence among the Sisters to draw them to join in the undertaking. One young professed Sister acceded to her wishes and left the community. Mother St. Joseph, seeing the necessity for the immediate dismissal of the lady, requested her to leave the convent at her earliest convenience. Madame de Cercy heaped bitter reproaches upon her, threatened a lawsuit against the community for the recovery of her share of the purchase, and, as is usual in such cases, spoke in most unfavorable terms of the Mother and Sisters. The superior received this trial with her wonted calmness and resignation; and when some one told her that persons spoke evil against her on account of the proceeding, she answered: "All they can say can but bring me humiliation, which is necessary for me; and since the house of Talence is thus shaken by the storm, its foundation will stand every future trial."

CHAPTER XXXVIII.

HER ZEAL FOR THE OBSERVANCE OF RULE.

IN June, 1847, Mother St. Joseph derived great consolation from the visits of Bishops de la Croix and Depery. Both these prelates had successively been her superior, the one at Belley and the other at Gap. Bishop Depery had befriended her when all others abandoned her cause and regarded her as a subject for the insane asylum; moreover, it was partly through his influence that she was sent to Bordeaux. She was overjoyed to see both these friends, who had witnessed the most trying phases of her life, and she opened her soul and mind and communicated all her intentions to them. She fully appreciated the regard testified by their coming a distance to see her and the community;

while they were equally pleased at the good accomplished through her. Before leaving, they congratulated the archbishop on the progress of the congregation under his paternal care and direction. On his return to Gap Bishop Depery wrote to her: "I left Bordeaux with a heart full of grief and gratitude—grief because I was obliged to leave there, and gratitude for your welcome reception. I went there only to see you, and to be convinced that God wanted you in that country. His blessing attends your works, and I am certain He will not withdraw His hand, but will ever continue His protection over you. Labor to inculcate the interior spirit, having for a model St. Joseph in the house of Nazareth. Always keep his plane in your hands to level, arrange, and polish all the material given you."

The Mother's health could not be fully restored while she attended to the various duties that devolved upon her. The physicians prescribed a release from all care and absolute rest. They advised her to go to the Cataracts; but she objected, on account of the expense incident to the journey and stay there. Moreover, she was averse to absenting herself from the Sisters. All hesitation, however, was put an end to when the same course of treatment was prescribed for one of the Sisters in poor health.

Her confidence in St. Michael was so great that she desired to increase the practice of devotion to him, and with this view she composed a litany in his honor, and sent it to Bishop Devie for correction and approbation before having printed copies distributed. He wrote to her, and sent his second volume of explanations on the catechism and a selection of hymns. In his letter he says: "I have learned with pleasure that the desire of our hearts has been granted, and that the good God has restored your health. Continue to devote it entirely to His glory by doing all in your power towards establishing houses where He will be honored and served, and where others will be taught to know and love Him. Such works will open heaven's gates for us."

Exact observance of rule was a source of great anxiety to Mother St. Joseph. "Infractions of rule," she says, "are like openings in the roof or walls of a house—they insensibly lead to complete ruin." The slightest non-observance was punished with a severe reprimand and penance. If one violated any special point of rule, she showed a severity almost incredible in one whose heart was naturally tender and affectionate. On one occasion, when three Sisters were guilty of the violation of the rule forbidding them to take their meals in the houses of seculars where religious houses of their own order are established, she publicly imposed on one a deprivation of Holy Communion on any week-day during one year; another, who was a novice, she obliged to make an additional year of novitiate; and the third, who was in charge of the house, she reproached in bitter terms, telling her that no penance was severe enough to punish the fault, and she would leave her to God.

After the retreat in September, the archbishop received eight professions and gave the habit to eight novices. Besides the house at Talence, another was opened at Cussac in October of that year, to the great satisfaction of all concerned.

Towards the close of 1847 the good Mother seemed oppressed with a weight of sadness, and by constant prayer she strove to avert in a measure the storm she saw approaching and threatening the Church. One day she held in her hand a black stone which was brought her by a pilgrim from La Salette, and, while examining it, tears coursed down her cheeks, and her sadness seemed to increase. On a Sister asking the cause of her affliction, she replied: "I see our Holy Father the Pope leaving Rome." The Sisters assured her that Pius IX. reigned gloriously in Rome, and that no danger threatened him; but their efforts to console her were unavailing. Early in 1848 her fears increased still more after a vision she had, and which left a deep impression on her heart. One day, while in adoration before the Blessed Sacrament, our Lord appeared to her, holding in his hands a thunderbolt, which seemed on the point of being cast upon the earth. She became cold with terror, and besought our Lord to spare men and convert them, saying: "Lord, we are guilty and ungrateful, but we are redeemed by Thy precious blood, which is daily offered in sacrifice for us."

"My daughter," our divine Lord answered, "see how I am offended without ceasing; it seems that man is ever striving to invent new outrages against me."

"Yes, Lord," she pleaded; "but the sacrifice of expiation is likewise continual. When no more Masses, no sacrifice, to repair offences against you are offered, it will be time enough to punish."

"But even in the sacrament of love I am profaned and my love and mercy abused. How many Masses are celebrated and heard without piety or preparation, how many sacrilegious receptions of my body and blood occur, and how little regard is shown for my Presence in the Blessed Sacrament! What a marked difference between my house and the houses of the great ones of the earth! The one is often deserted, while the other is always surrounded and God is forgotten for creatures."

His suppliant still prayed: "See, Lord, how many souls sacrifice themselves for your love and glory. I offer all these to you in reparation for those who do not love you;

and, Jesus, I offer the love of your own Heart in the tabernacle, and that of your immaculate Mother Mary, for guilty man. Redeemer of mankind, have mercy on us!" Our Lord disappeared, and His servant resolved to doall in her power in reparation for the outrages offered Jesus in the Blessed Sacrament.

The good Mother related this vision to the Sisters, and all commenced a novena in honor of the love of Jesus shown in the sacramental Presence. During nine months there were constant adorers before the Blessed Sacrament, and once a month, by special permission of the archbishop, exposition of the Blessed Sacrament was granted for twenty-four hours. The pious superior spent all the time not claimed by other duties before the Blessed Sacrament, and when called away her heart and thoughts remained with Jesus in the tabernacle. All the Sisters united in the performance of acts of penance and sacrifice to appease the wrath of God; and as all shared in their Mother's sentiments, never was there more fervor and more devotion to the Real Presence. When they heard of the flight of our Holy Father into Gaeta, their hearts were imbued with sorrow; and they increased their fervor in prayer, and petitioned with unwearied perseverance for the triumph of our holy Church. The Mother not only constantly exhorted the Sisters, but also prayed persons of the world to communicate more frequently and to spend more time before God in prayer. She recommended the use of the ejaculatory prayer then so little known: "Eternal Father, I offer Thee the precious blood of Jesus Christ, Thy divine Son, in expiation for my sins, for the wants of the Church, the conversion of sinners, and the deliverance of the souls in purgatory."

No one can tell how much the prayers offered by the whole Catholic Church at that period of trial and threatened troubles effected towards averting the wrath of God and securing the great Pontiff Pius IX. from danger.

CHAPTER XXXIX.

LETTERS OF BISHOP DEVIE—MOTHER ST. JOSEPH VISITS BOURG, BELLEY, AND ARS.

THE political disturbance of 1848 lessened the number of applicants for admission into religious orders. On the Feast of the Visitation that year but four postulants received the habit; and after the retreat in September, nine made their profession and but one postulant was received.

On the 2d of December a letter from Bishop Devie tells Mother St. Joseph that the Sisters at Bourg are in great alarm on account of the troubles in the town; he advises her to take all prudent measures towards securing her establishments at Belley, and to make a will in favor of some reliable person who would carry out her intentions. "As for yourself," he said, "I understand you are not disturbed; that you are even increasing the number of your houses, and praying with fervor. May God be blessed and glorified, and may His graces be daily increased for yourself and your daughters! This is my constant petition, offered in union with your prayers and good works."

Mother St. Joseph was deeply moved on reading this letter from her spiritual father, and on the 7th of December she replied that she was disposed to do all in her power to secure the foundations at Belley; that she had confided the care of them to a person who she knew would carry into effect even her least wishes. With regard to the Sisters, she said they were truly fervent; the religious spirit reigned among them, and she attributed this favor to his prayers, the direction of their good superior, Father Taillefer, and the paternal solicitude of the archbishop.

Early in 1849 the good Mother became acquainted with Miss Clara Auriemma, who labored to spread devotion to the most Blessed Sacrament of the Altar. These two holy souls soon understood each other, and formed an intimate union which was interrupted only by the death of Mother St. Joseph, though continued in the person of her successor and the religious of the Congregation of St. Joseph. The work propagated by this young girl met with the fullest approbation of Mother St. Joseph. After the departure of Clara, on the 17th of March, she wrote to Father Conlin, director of the work: "Although I have not the honor of acquaintance with you, I take the liberty of congratulating you on the noble and holy undertaking you have commenced. What is more sublime and conducive to the good of souls than perpetual adoration of the Blessed Sacrament? This has been the dream of my life. I heard of the institution of the Living Rosary, and I experienced pain in not hearing of devotion to the Son, hidden in the lowly tabernacle, at the same time with devotion to the Mother. However, I sincerely love the Blessed Virgin, and the innumerable graces I have received through her intercession force me to feel confidence in, and love for, her. But I wish that while forming an association in France for the purpose of honoring Mary, the promoters would establish another by which devotion to the most Blessed Sacrament would be increased. You are, then, dear father, the means destined by God from all eternity to propagate this devotion, which will, I trust, convert more souls than could many missionaries.

"When our Lord lived on earth, the Gospel tells us that those who approached Him received an abundance of favors and graces, and never asked in vain. Would that souls were well penetrated with the truth of this assurance! They could then realize that He still dwells among them, hidden in the tabernacle, as truly as when he walked with men, and that He is as willing now as then to hear our prayers and relieve our wants. I entreat that amiable Prisoner of Love to inspire all hearts with this devotion, and make them docile to the inspirations of His grace. I believe the secret of this devotion to be love of the cross and humiliation."

Father Conlin answered as follows: "Your letter is a source of great consolation to me. May God be blessed a thousand thousand times! I agree with you in your sentiments. It is indeed Jesus Christ who is the principle and the end of all devotion. This is forgotten even among pious persons, because they do not meditate on the Real Presence. Many find devotion in pictures and popular devotions which attract the imagination for a while, but fail to bring the desired end. Why is the Blessed Sacrament so little spoken of? We see priests who spend months and years in a town, and they scarcely ever speak of the Blessed Sacrament, except in exhorting to receive the Holy Communion; as if Jesus in the tabernacle, in His sacred humanity, were not the mainspring of all good. Let us pray most fervently that a change in this particular may be effected."

In the following month of April Mother St. Joseph undertook a journey to Lyons to attend to business concerning her community. From thence she went to Belley to visit Mother St. Regis, who had been her superior at Chazay. As Bishop Devie was absent from Belley, Mother St. Joseph went to Bourg in the hope of seeing him there, and at the same time in acceptance of a pressing invitation from Mother St. Claude, who always entertained the greatest regard for her. Her hope of meeting the bishop there was realized, and, as both had a presentiment that this was to be their last meeting on earth, they mutually promised an interchange of prayers for a happy death.

No change was made in the administration of the house at Belley, notwithstanding the wishes of the bishop to that effect; but as important repairs had been recently made, she promised to send fifty-five hundred francs to the superior-general of Bourg. She also visited the holy curé of Ars, whose generous soul was congenial to her. He still lamented the cherished Providence of which he had been deprived, and spoke feelingly of the regret with which its inmates bade adieu to its protecting walls. "But," he added, "the good God wanted that house. I now attend to missions and instruct souls wandering in error's path; and you establish houses wherein God will be glorified." He listened with great interest to all she related about the novitiate at Bordeaux, and he promised to pray God to bless the work still more. He had already sent many postulants to her, and continued during her life to send them. When some expressed fears of not being admitted on account of want of means, he said: "Have no fears; go to Bordeaux, and Mother St. Joseph will receive you as you are."

On Mother St. Joseph's return she found four postulants ready to receive the habit. She caused preparations to be made for the holding of the ceremony, which took place in May, 1849.

In a letter dated June 4, Bishop Devie reminded her of the promise of fifty-five hundred francs to be given to Mother St. Claude. He again referred to the Providence in Belley, and closed his letter with:

"You appeared surprised at your last visit to find your old father in full possession of his memory and energy; pray now that he may make a holy use of these faculties, for it often happens that one's mind, and with it good-will, imperceptibly fails with years. Let us make good use of the time yet allowed us to prepare for

eternity; let us neglect nothing to accomplish the designs of God in our regard, but be well persuaded that of ourselves we can do no good, being mere instruments in the hands of Providence. I will be pleased to read the notes you are taking preparatory to having your custom-book finished. Write whatever you deem best, and I will communicate to you all my observations on them. I remain, in union with the Sacred Hearts of Jesus and Mary,
"Yours in Christ,
"A. DEVIE, Bishop."

Mother St. Joseph did not comply with his wishes concerning the final disposition of the Goux estate. Although she revered the bishop as a saint, she could not bring herself to obey his wishes in this particular, and she applied for advice in the matter to an eminent theologian, who counselled her to remain firm in her refusal of the proposed absolute change in the conditions made in the transfer of 1840. Bishop Devie wished her to give him the right to use the revenue for the benefit of the congregation at Bourg, and to assume all responsibility himself in the disposition of it. This Mother St. Joseph refused, as such an arrangement would be in direct opposition to the intention of the donor.

About this time she learned that a colony of Sisters of St. Joseph at Annecy had undertaken the foundation of a house in the Indies, for the purpose of aiding the Catholic missionaries. As before stated, Mother St. Joseph had made a conditional vow to devote her life to the service of God in the Indies; but her superiors were opposed to her fulfilment of this vow, and, with the view of assisting as much as in her power, she constantly prayed for the success of the laborers there, and of increase of faith among them. Immediately on hearing of the projected mission, she wrote to the superior at Annecy, asking permission to be allowed the privilege of furnishing the outfit for the Sisters; and on receiving an affirmative answer, she paid the expenses of the voyage and furnished all she deemed necessary for them to commence their labors in their distant mission. After attending to this self-imposed duty, she went to spend a week at the Cataracts, in obedience to the wishes of the archbishop, who desired the recovery of her strength, which had been impaired by travelling.

During her absence the four missionaries of St. Francis de Sales visited Bordeaux and stopped at the convent. Kindest attentions were bestowed on the Sisters during their stay, and they left for the Indies, their hearts filled with gratitude towards Mother St. Joseph and her daughters. Since that time an intimate union of sentiment and prayer exists between the Sisters of St. Joseph of Annecy and of Bordeaux.

On her way to the watering-place, which she visited every year until her death, she stopped at Auch to see Bishop de la Croix. This worthy bishop had written to her that she would always meet with a welcome for herself and companion, and assured her that he never forgot her in his prayers, but always recommended herself, her works, and her community to the good God. He could not forget the superior of Belley and of Gap.

While at the watering-place she performed her spiritual exercises at the time appointed by rule. She arose before daylight, assisted at Mass, and received Holy Communion. All her spare time was occupied in the performance of acts of charity. Many persons were inspired with confidence in her at first sight, and sought counsel of her in their miseries and doubts. When her means were expended, she solicited aid for the poor from those more favored in temporal wealth. On one occasion she gave her chair to a poor soldier who was too weak to ascend the stairs, and begged others to carry him up and down when required. On learning that for want of means he thought of leaving before a cure was effected, she supplied him with the necessary amount. Her charity was extended to all, and God rewarded it by her restoration to health.

The house at Bordeaux became too small for the number of Sisters and postulants. The cholera was raging in the city, and fear of the epidemic made the Sisters still more anxious for a more commodious house. It was proposed to build a separate edifice at some distance from the one occupied, but on the same grounds; and after submitting the plans and specifications to the archbishop for approval, the building was about to be commenced, when one of the criminals she had converted at Gap appeared to her in a vision and told her to desist from this purpose, as God destined a more suitable house for the community. On the same night St. Philomena gave the same communication to one of the Sisters. The project was abandoned, Mother St. Joseph awaited with patience the will of divine Providence, and the Sisters were fearless of the scourge.

The cholera continued to make other victims, and the pious superior addressed the following circular to all the houses of the congregation: "My dear daughters, you lament with us over the great scourge that afflicts France. At all times God has given to His people a dread of the cholera, in order to bring back to the fold sheep who were straying from it. Let us, my dear children, make use of this fear, and return sincerely in spirit and in truth to God. Strive to avert the scourge by a spirit of compunction, by prayer, and above all by an exact observance of our holy rule.

These are the most efficacious means to keep the epidemic from among us. Join to exact observance fervent prayers in honor of the Blessed Virgin and our holy father St. Joseph. You may add a Pater and Ave in honor of St. Roch, and repeat an invocation to him. Pray also for the conversion of sinners, that they may repent sincerely for their sins, and be prepared to receive a favorable sentence from the merciful and just Judge of all. Consider that the precious blood of Jesus Christ was shed for mankind in general and for each in particular. It is, then, in honor of this adorable blood that we pray with all possible fervor to obtain a happy death for the victims of cholera or any epidemic."

After the general retreat in September, three received the habit and five made their profession; and again, in December, four received the habit and one made her profession.

Several foundations were asked for, but the Mother established those only which the bishop required at St. Vivien and Vendays.

CHAPTER XL.

NEW EDITION OF RULES.

THE year 1850 opened under the most favorable auspices. Applications were made for the establishment of houses in all parts of the diocese, the number of postulants was greatly increased, and on the 19th of March, feast of the patron of the congregation, five received the habit of the order. Notwithstanding the multifarious duties consequent on her charge of the interior of the convent, her usual charities were, as of old, exercised abroad, and this year she herself obtained the admission of three young boys into the order of the Christian Brothers, and two others into a seminary.

On the 22d of April she was subjected to a new trial in the death of Sister St.

Francis Xavier, who died at the early age of twenty-four years, after a long and painful illness, borne with heroic patience and fortitude. Some hours before her death the Sister said: "I could never have believed the approach of death would bring me so great happiness. Mother, give me some cause for humiliation." A few moments afterwards she raised herself in the bed, took holy water, turned her eyes towards heaven, and died pressing the crucifix to her lips.

The supply of the Constitutions brought to Bordeaux being exhausted, and a new one needed, the foundress resolved on having a new edition printed, in which a few modifications were made, such as the changes brought about in the lapse of two hundred years and acknowledged customs rendered necessary. This work she submitted for examination to the provincial council at Bordeaux in July, 1850, and it received the unanimous approval of the ten bishops who composed the council, all of whom affixed their signatures to the manuscript.

In September of the same year she

learned that the Hôtel Calvimont was offered for sale. This hotel, located in the central part of the city, near the cathedral, occupied extensive grounds, and the surroundings were specially adapted to the wants of a religious community. The archbishop immediately sent Mother St. Joseph to Paris to make arrangements with the owner of the property for its purchase. This was her first visit to Paris, and while there she spent all the time her business transactions allowed in the Church of Our Lady of Victory. On being requested to examine and admire the magnificent monuments of kingly grandeur with which art had embellished the city, she replied: "To me now there is nothing more beautiful than heaven. I will go to Our Lady of Victory, as I have still a favor to ask there." There in that sanctuary, in the midst of hundreds who fervently offered their petitions to God and his holy Mother, she found happiness, and placed her children and the future of her congregation, as well as the affair that brought her to Paris, in the hands of the Virgin Mother Mary. After serious reflection, she decided on having the title to the property obtained for the community, and returned to Bordeaux.

A journey from Paris was in those days a much greater undertaking than at present, and was consequently attended with great fatigue to Mother St. Joseph, whose health at that time was in a weak state. Nevertheless, as the general retreat had commenced, on her return she was allowed no time to rest, and was at all times accessible to the Sisters who wished to speak to her, and entered into their wants and spiritual necessities with unremitting zeal. She had many prayers and good works offered to God for the success of the projected work, which she knew would be a great acquisition to the congregation.

At the close of this retreat nine postulants received the habit, and four new foundations were made in the diocese— at Berlin, Lamargue, Leognen, and St. Selve. The two former houses were opened under the auspices of the respective mayors, M. Tabre and M. Canteau, and the two latter at the request of the parish priests, Fathers Taillardat and Grimal, and with the temporal assistance of Madame de Canole and Count Etchegoyen.

The sale of the hotel was concluded on the 5th of November, and deeded to Mother St. Joseph for one hundred and twenty thousand francs. This sum, with the expenses attendant on the transaction, was much larger than was actually at her command; but her faith in Providence, as usual, came to her aid. With her wonted confidence, she tried human means; and when they failed to supply necessary resources, she appealed to God.

On the 21st of November she was called upon for the payment of eleven thousand five hundred francs; but with all her efforts she succeeded in securing only fifty-five hundred. Without, however, allowing herself the least uneasiness, she went to the foot of the altar and said: "My divine Master, I have tried all available human means, and failed. I come now to you, who never refuse anything to those who ask with confidence." She then told a Sister to go to the door and introduce the first person who should come. In the course of an hour an old gentleman, who known on account of his wealth, came to the door. The Sister said to him: "Mother is waiting to see you. Please go to her."

"You must be mistaken," replied the visitor; "for I am not acquainted with your superior. She cannot be waiting to see me."

He went up-stairs, however, as he had come with the intention of seeing Mother St. Joseph. When she told him the cause of her embarrassment, he said: "Go immediately to the office, and I will return to my house for six thousand francs, and will follow you with it."

He did so, and would not even take a receipt. Later this worthy gentleman lent ninety-seven thousand francs to complete the payment on the hotel, and gave the community its own time to return the sum to him.

Having thus provided for the future temporal wants of the community, the good Mother wished to ensure its spiritual perpetuity, and obtain, if possible, the approval of the Constitutions by our Holy Father Pius IX. She was desirous to go herself to Rome for the purpose, but numerous obstacles in her way deterred her. An ablegate, who had been commissioned with the beretta of the Cardinal of Austria, and had spent some days at the archiepiscopal palace of Bordeaux, was requested by his grace Mgr. Donnet to present the Constitutions for the approval of the Holy Father. "My old age," she wrote, "would be happy if, before closing my eyes to the darkness of this life to open them on eternal light, I could say, 'Lord, let your servant now depart in peace, since her children are placed in the bark of Peter to remain for ever.'"

Until this time the existence of the Sisters of St. Joseph at Bordeaux was not recognized by the government, but depended on the congregation of Bourg for any legal transactions with the Academy. Mother St. Joseph was anxious to secure all privileges for her order, and to see it solidly established in the city. She accordingly asked its recognition by the state in a letter dated January 8, 1851, wherein it was stated that the institute had already eighteen establishments in the department of the Gironde and the neighborhood. The municipal council granted the requested favor on March 10, 1851, and, through the favor and great influence of Archbishop Donnet with the prefect, a decree was given, October 23, 1852, acknowledging the Sisters of St. Joseph at Bordeaux as a congregation directed by a superior-general.

Although engaged in the enterprise above mentioned, Mother St. Joseph's care and attention were bestowed on the removal of the novitiate. The last reception at the court of Aquitaine took place on the 30th of March, 1851, and on the 1st of May following the whole community were assembled in the Hôtel Calvimont.

The chapel was found entirely inadequate to the number of Sisters, and one of the good Mother's first projects was to build a chapel large enough to accommodate not only the present community, but all those in the future whom faith showed her ranged in that novitiate under the pennant of St. Joseph. At the same time she expressed a hope that the walls of the interior would be decorated with paintings traced by their own hands. "God," she said, "will be pleased with their good will; the angels can add finishing touches. Good desires are always most agreeable in the divine eyes." Having no means at her disposal for the erection of a chapel, she determined to sacrifice to this purpose a magnificent figure of Christ carved in ivory, and said to be the work of one of the old masters. Her old benefactor, M. Pasquier, of Lyons, had sent it to her as a gift. After obtaining his permission to dispose of it, she sent the figure to Paris, where it was bought by Madame Chatelet for ten thousand francs. This generous lady made an offering of her purchase to Pius IX. This destination amply compensated her for any sacrifice the parting with the figure had cost her. The Holy Father sent her his apostolic benediction, and she often took pleasure in uniting her sentiments with those he experienced in passing before that image of Jesus crucified.

As soon as Mother St. Joseph received the money, the building was commenced. The archbishop, accompanied by several clergy, laid the corner-stone on the 2d of

August, 1851, and the chapel was finished in 1852. It was built in Corinthian style, and no expense was spared to make it a fitting habitation for the divine Presence.

Mother St. Joseph was now happy in the possession of a convent large enough for a general assembly of the Sisters, and which would serve as a home for them. "Be grateful to Him," she said, "who has given you so large a house and a country so beautiful. He can never be outdone in generosity; but He is content with our fullest love. Let us, then, love and serve Him by our fidelity to our vows and our holy rule, by our zeal for the salvation of souls, by our humility—which convinces us that, though we do all things, still we are useless servants—and by our charity towards our neighbor; for by these we will have fulfilled the law."

She wished each Sister to know the distribution which she proposed to make in the house, and she was filled with almost childlike delight on seeing the pleasure the Sisters evinced in listening to her details. "My children," she said, "your happiness is mine. I desire but one thing, which is, that your rest here may be succeeded by an eternal rest in heaven. It is impossible for me to pray here below as much as I would wish. I long to see everything progress well, that the good God may take me to Himself, where I shall pray incessantly for my well-beloved ones."

Her charity increased as the claimants to its exercise increased. Each one sincerely manifested the state of her soul to her without a thought of intrusion. When they had finished, she always asked: "My child, are you perfectly content with what you have said? Is nothing else a source of trouble to you?"

When the Sisters who communicated with her had a will to speak with simplicity and sincerity, God allowed her to feel a great sweetness. She read their souls with as much readiness as a book, and she conversed a long time without fatigue. When, on the contrary, Sisters were wanting in sincerity towards her, she experienced weariness, and could not fix her attention on what they said, nor could she find wherewith to answer them.

Sometimes, however, enlightened by God, she said: "My child, you have not the courage to make yourself known to me as you really know yourself. I tell you from myself that such is the case."

On one occasion, after being long occupied in this manner, a Sister said to her: "Mother, I know you are tired."

"Oh! no," she replied. "When I find Sisters open, candid, and confiding, and with a sincere desire to advance in virtue, nothing will fatigue me. Even grave faults, when well known and simply acknowledged, can be overcome, and we have a right to hope all from the goodness of God and a firm will, to which candid avowal gives great strength."

The good Mother watched with no less solicitude over the temporal wants of her children. She herself had a spirit of rigorous mortification, and she carefully cultivated and preserved it in her community; but when the practice was in the least injurious to their health, she moderated it, and always directed each as her strength would permit, and this with a care that only truly maternal affection could have inspired. She studied the physical constitution of each Sister, and would not suffer the slightest indisposition to pass unnoticed or unattended. The lungs particularly, so easily affected by prolonged and continual teaching, she made an object of especial care, and she provided each house with a supply of cod-liver oil, to be used in case of necessity. If she heard a Sister cough in the chapel in the morning, she would wait at the door until the exercise was over, and, as the Sisters passed, would stop the one who had been the object of her attention, and examine if her clothing was comfortable and warm, and always gave particular orders that warm hose and thick-soled shoes be provided, besides prescribing other remedies. Those in poor health were an object of special care to her, and she employed them in light duties suitable to their age and temperament. No one was slighted, or offended, or jealous; for the Sisters knew that all were equally beloved by her, and that each, under like circumstances, would receive the same treatment.

Mother St. Joseph had, however, a preference for lay Sisters. She said that, as there is nothing in their employment calculated to nourish self-love, when they have the spirit of good religious they can with facility acquire humility, and then, being perfectly disengaged from terrestrial objects, God will suffuse their souls with ineffable delight. For the rest, there was perfect equality in the house—not the least difference in food, material for habits, prayers, recreations, and other exercises of the lay Sisters from the others. The postulants were never told which habit was to be given them until their reception, on the evening preceding which they were asked if they had any objection or dislike to receiving the lay habit. If any reason existed for supposing a postulant averse to becoming a lay Sister, the Mother unhesitatingly deferred her reception, and even dismissed some and sent them back to the world. "Better," she said, "to have a small number of Sisters who sincerely wish to humble themselves than a great many proud ones." All in the house were occupied alike in manual labor and the humblest employments.

At the close of the retreat, on the 14th of October, 1851, nine made their profession and six received the habit. After this, three new foundations were made—one at Virelade, the expenses of which were defrayed by Madame Joseph Carrayon La Tour; the second at Pessac, where a school and orphan asylum were placed under the care of the Sisters (in a short time two hundred orphans were sheltered within its hospitable walls); the third at ———.

CHAPTER XLI.

LAST GENERAL RETREAT PRESIDED OVER BY MOTHER ST. JOSEPH—HER LAST ILLNESS AND DEATH.

THE new house built by Mother St. Joseph was sufficiently large to accommodate a great number of young postulants. Nine received the habit, and five made their profession at the hands of the archbishop, who was about to leave for Rome, where he was to be consecrated cardinal, under the title of St. Mary in Via. The news of this promotion greatly rejoiced the heart of the good Mother; for she always entertained sentiments of lively gratitude towards him on account of the many personal favors conferred on her and the great interes the manifested in her works.

Shortly after this reception, Mother St. Joseph undertook to make the usual annual visitation. She considered it of the greatest importance to visit each of the houses at least once a year. She commissioned this duty to one of the elder Sisters when she herself was unable to fulfil it—which, however, was very seldom. She frequently made these visitations unannounced, so as to see at a glance if the state of affairs was in conformity with the holy rule and her private instructions. Each Sister rendered an account of her interior dispositions, of the state of her health, and the customs of the house. The good Mother visited the classes, examined the children's copy-books, and assured herself as to the observance of order, cleanliness, and silence. She used to say that the progress of the pupils depended on the good discipline of the school.

Mother St. Joseph also examined into the relations of the communities with externs. She wished the Sisters to always speak of and act with the greatest-respect towards parish priests. "You are here," she said, "to aid them in the salvation of souls. You ought never to join in complaints against them, nor ever listen to any. If it should happen that you are forced to hear such, it is your duty to conciliate those who make them, and excite the confidence of all, particularly the children under your care, in the ministers of God. Act in the same way towards all priests. Say nothing against them; even should you imagine there is cause for blame, it is your place to keep silent." She prudently retrenched useless visits.

Mother St. Joseph was on one occasion very much pleased on learning that the Sisters at an establishment of five years' standing had never been abroad, except when charity or necessity required.

She wished also due respect to be paid to the public officers and the school inspectors. "They are," she said, "representatives of authority, and we ought to obey them when they ask nothing contrary to our rules or the glory of God."

This visitation greatly impaired the health of Mother St. Joseph. But the waters of the Cataracts, where she spent the month of July, restored her vigor a little. On her return to Bordeaux she learned at Auch, from Bishop de la Croix, of the death of

Bishop Devie. She was so greatly afflicted at the announcement that she could not continue her journey until the next day. She mingled her tears with those of Bishop de la Croix, who was an intimate friend of the great prelate, whose death the Church of France deplored. Letters from Father Robert, canon of Belley, and from Father Colletta, which she received a few days after, brought her the sad consolation of a detailed account of his death, and also of the honors paid his memory by the clergy and the faithful.

At the general retreat held in the month of September, the last at which the pious foundress presided, she repeated her instructions with an energy and zeal that told without a doubt of her expectation of death.

It was customary, on the arrival of the Sisters at the novitiate to spend the vacation, for the local superiors to resume their places according to date of profession. The Sisters then had but one superior. All were equally ignorant of their destination the coming year, and, indeed, gave themselves no uneasiness in the matter. When, at the close of the retreat, each one was assigned her post, it was found that superiors were often called to take the lowest employments, and Sisters were removed from one house to another in the diocese. No one, however, complained, but cheerfully followed the order of obedience, and willingly executed the duties assigned her.

Each Sister, on her return to the noviciate, took with her whatever was furnished for her use. The good Mother made a general examination of the clothing, the books, and all the articles belonging to them, that she might replace those unfit for use, deprive them of what might be superfluous, and ascertain if all was in conformity with the requirement of holy rule. She frequently obliged the Sisters to exchange books, etc., with no other intention in view than to cultivate among them the spirit of detachment and poverty.

Mother St. Joseph insisted more forcibly than ever on the practice of union and charity. "All could be said in two words, and these words should be graven everywhere. Write them on your hearts; make them the subject of your habitual reflections and the invariable rule of your life; these two words are, mutual support. Yes, my dear children, with mutual aid the bond of your lives, all will go on well, and the religious life will be a foretaste of heaven." She earnestly recommended the custom of praying for the church and her supreme head, giving as a rule never to assist at the holy sacrifice of the Mass or receive Holy Communion without praying for the Sovereign Pontiff. The community said the Rosary every Sunday—one part for the Holy Father, another for the archbishop and all the clergy, and the third to obtain for all the Sisters the grace of a happy death.

After this retreat, six were received as novices; and six made their vows. A few months later two new foundations were made—one at Begadan and the other at Sancats.

As yet but two Sisters had died since the establishment at Bordeaux. On the 13th of June death claimed a third victim in Sister Leopold, who was distinguished for her untiring charity towards the sick. Again the good Mother's heart bled with sorrow on the death of Sister St. Paul, who died at the age of fifty-two years. The example of this holy religious was to the community like a sweet, heavenly perfume, wafting virtue to their souls. Her great happiness was found in the practice of unlimited obedience. She edified the young novices by her humility, her sweetness, her indulgence towards others in time of trial—which had its source in charity—and her spirit of obedience, that led her to ask even the smallest permissions with a persevering and faithful exactitude. Mother St. Joseph found consolation in this loss only in the thought that they would soon meet in eternity, never to know separation. Her health visibly declined from day to day, but the energy of her will supplied strength, and she did not in the least moderate her wonted efforts to prepare the novices and postulants for the approaching ceremony, which took place on the 17th of April, when five made their profession and eight received the habit.

The unbounded joy Mother St. Joseph experienced in the following month of June on the arrival at Bordeaux of a colony of

Missionaries of St. Francis de Sales and the Sisters of St. Joseph at Annecy, on their way to the Indies, seemed to restore for a time all the ardor of her youth. She spoke of the sublimity of their vocation with an extraordinary warmth of soul, and she prepared all that was necessary for their journey, as if she felt neither weakness nor sufferings. But after their departure she fell into a state of dejection and debility. The Sisters became alarmed at the state of her health. They recalled to mind the words of Father Bonet. She herself had said before leaving the house in the court of Aquitaine, when one day they begged her to take more care of her health: " My children, I will not die until you have a suitable home and chapel and the work of God be well advanced."

For some years, too, she had spoken of her coming death. In 1849 she wrote to M. Guillomot, vicar-general of Belley: " I feel that I am going at a rapid pace." On the day of the purchase of the Hôtel Calvimont, in the midst of the joy that filled the hearts of the religious, she said: " My children, the term of my pilgrimage is near at hand. As soon as you are well provided for and have a chapel, I will leave you for eternity."

Although she was far advanced in years, the Sisters hoped the waters of the Cataracts would restore her strength this time, as in preceding years. She went there in July with her old friend Father Colletta, who had come to see her.

At this time Mother St. Joseph was subjected to great interior trials. During the last days of 1853 her soul was deprived of the usual sweetness and divine communication in prayer with which God had favored her. At meditation she was assailed with doubts, fears, and temptations of all kinds. Her heart seemed cold and hard, and she was oppressed with sadness. "I fear," she said to Sister Conception, "that God has abandoned me on account of some hidden sin." The first attack of sickness brought comparative calm; for she was always willing to endure bodily pains. "What," she said, "are corporal sufferings in comparison with those of the soul?"

After a few days at the Cataracts, she recovered her strength, and with it all the spiritual joy, interior peace, and intimate union of her heart with Jesus Christ returned. The flood of grace seemed to flow into her soul with the force and rapidity of pent-up waters. Divine love inundated her heart, and her exhortations to love Jesus hidden in the tabernacle, and to beg Him to listen to our petitions and relieve our necessities, were so earnest that those she addressed were moved to tears.

One day, while going up to the railing with Sister Conception, whose health was always very feeble, the Sister was seized with a violent attack of sickness, and fears for her life were entertained. Her extremities were cold, and her countenance pale and ghastly. The good Mother, whose affection for the Sister had never diminished, made a vow to Our Lady of La Salette, and besought our Lord to shorten her own life, but spare that of her dear companion. This prayer was heard; the Sister was soon restored to consciousness, and in a few days recovered her usual health so far as to be able to fulfil the vow made to the Blessed Virgin. On the Feast of St. Anne following, the good Mother went, as was her morning custom, to the railing, without feeling in the least indisposed. But in the afternoon she was taken with a violent attack of fever, and the physician pronounced her illness serious. All the Sisters at once prayed incessantly for her restoration to health, but the petition was not granted them. However, she recovered strength sufficient to enable her to return to Bordeaux. When she found herself once more at home, surrounded by her community, her countenance beamed with such happiness that no one could believe she suffered as in reality she did suffer. The religious prayed with so much fervor and confidence that they were certain of her restoration to health. Communions, extraordinary penances, Masses celebrated in sanctuaries specially consecrated to Mary, conditional vows—nothing was neglected. Her patience did not desert her for an instant. It happened sometimes, despite their efforts to the contrary, that skin was pulled off with the blisters; but she never showed the least impatience in the suffering. When the Sisters expressed pity for her, she said: "What is all this? In heaven we will see God, will chant His praises, and our joy will be proportionate to the sufferings endured here below for His love." She asked the smallest permission from the infirmarian; not even the most fervent novice could have been more exact. She always had a pleasant, good word and gracious smile for the Sisters who came to see her. When she could speak, she gave a short sentence to each, which they received as a special rule suited to the disposition of their souls: "My child, you will make great progress in the spiritual life if you are faithful in small observances." "Do the will of God in all things, and He will fulfil whatever you wish." "All passes; God alone is eternal." "Nothing is difficult to a good will and by the grace of God." "Speak often of our Lord." "Out of the abundance of the heart the mouth speaks." "Console yourselves; life is short. We will soon be reunited. Sufferings are the gate to heaven." When the Sisters came in great numbers to spend the vacation and make their general retreat, she said to them: "You are happy to return to the novitiate, and you have reason to be; the novitiate is the vestibule of heaven. Be always faithful to your vocation; it is the greatest grace God could bestow on you." Her most frequent recommendation was: "My children, love one another." Knowing herself to be tenderly beloved by the Sisters, she feared that this affection was sometimes the only motive that actuated them in the fulfilment of their duties, and she said: "My children, I know I cause you much trouble and annoyance, but do all for God; let nothing human glide into your intentions; do not lose on my account the means given you by the good God to acquire treasures for heaven."

The strange physician who had been called in consultation was of the same opinion as the doctor of the house—that there was no possible hope of her recovery. But the Sisters would not listen to this decision. All the congregation were then united, and they commenced a perpetual adoration. Nine Sisters successively took their places at the foot of the tabernacle, and each offered her life in sacrifice for the recovery of their well-beloved Mother.

On the 18th of September the new chapel

was consecrated by Bishop Dupuch. Mother St. Joseph, who desired to have this ceremony take place before her death, was greatly consoled. The general retreat commenced on the same day, and, notwithstanding her extreme weakness, she prayed incessantly that God would favor these holy exercises with His divine blessing.

On the Feast of St. Michael the Sisters renewed their hopes, and invoked the intercession of this glorious archangel, towards whom the Mother entertained special devotion, and had frequently invoked with success. They begged her to unite with them in their prayers, and herself to ask for her recovery; and the superior, Father Taillefer, when giving her the Holy Communion at midnight, seconded the desire of the Sisters. She said the prayers desired of her, but added: " Lord, Thy will be done." On the same day his Eminence Cardinal Donnet came, as usual at the close of retreats. He had frequently visited her during her illness. In this visit he spoke to her of the good effected by the Sisters in the different parishes of the diocese, and told her to thank God for the good spirit which animated them. She could reply only: "Thank you, bishop; you will be always their father"; but tears of gratitude bedewed her cheeks as she uttered the words. In the evening she asked and received the last sacraments with sentiments of most lively faith. Two days before her death she became speechless. Her great sufferings drew from her sighs that pierced the souls of her attendants; but she prayed constantly, and followed the office of the Immaculate Conception, which the Sisters recited near her bed. Her heart was intimately united with Jesus crucified, and with Mary, the mother of sorrows; her eyes were fixed on their images, placed at the foot of her bed, and it might have been said she spoke to them.

At six o'clock on the morning of October 7, 1854, all the Sisters assembled around her bed to see her soul take its final leave of earth. They read the recommendation of the soul departing and said the daily morning prayers. It was evident, from the movement of her lips and the joyous expression of her countenance, that she took an attentive part in them. At half-past six

Sister Immaculate Conception, taking her hand, said: "Take courage, Mother; your hour is come. You are going to Jesus, whom your heart has ever loved. Be happy. We have courage to continue your work. Jesus, be to her a Saviour!" At these words an angelic smile suffused her features, and she slept peacefully in the Lord at the age of fifty-eight years.

Death did not change her countenance. It might have been said that it expressed a hitherto hidden freshness and beauty imparted to it by her many and heavenly virtues. Many of the Sisters felt an interior movement of joy, and could not refrain from saying: "Injustice to our good Mother could alone induce us to hold her captive, when we know she will aid us the more in heaven."

Their joy was followed by sorrow and lamentations, which were echoed from all sides. Adoring the secret judgments of God in regard to their Mother, the Sisters lost no time in procuring a great number of suffrages of our holy Church, and applying all indulgences and good works to her soul. But while their piety supplied these, they had an assurance that her soul was in possession of eternal bliss in the presence of its Creator.

On the 8th of October, the day after her death, and before its announcement was made at Bordeaux, a young lady, who afterwards became a religious under the name of Sister Eleanora, went to Ars and asked Father Vianney to offer a Mass for the recovery of Mother St. Joseph. The holy curé, smiling, said to her: "My child, she does not need it; she is dead." And he refused to say the Mass.

The spirit of this good religious lives to-day in her community. Her spiritual children still converse with her in prayer, claim her protection, and follow her counsels as faithfully as if she were with them. Without desiring or daring to anticipate the judgment of our holy mother the Church, they cannot refrain from attributing to the protection of their venerable foundress, outside a great number of personal favors, the progress of their congregation, the continuance of the spirit of obedience and sweet, mutual charity, which constitutes the happiness of the religious life, and is the unmistakable mark of the true Spirit of God.

Such were the life and works of Mother St. Joseph. When we consider altogether the fifty-eight years so well and admirably spent, we must feel that she had a right to exclaim in her last moments with the holy Apostle: "I have fought a good fight; I have finished my course; I have kept the faith. And for the rest, there is laid up for me a crown, which the Lord the just Judge will render unto me." May the lessons of this life implant the germs of virtue in souls and animate them to good resolutions!

APPENDIX.

I.

THE secular Sisters of St. Joseph were established at Bordeaux by Marie Delpech de l'Estang, who, assisted by some young girls and widows, undertook of themselves to educate a number of orphans. Cardinal Henry Escoubleau approved, on the 16th of June, 1638, a congregation under the title of "Society of Sisters of St. Joseph for the Care of Orphans." They made only a simple vow of obedience, but they maintained among themselves a spirit of poverty, and did not apply their revenue to their own particular use. The cardinal gave them new constitutions in 1652, which were confirmed in 1694 by Bishop Louis Anglare, of Bourlemont. Louis XIII. confirmed their establishment by letters-patent in 1639, and Louis XIV. by letter in

May, 1673. The houses at that time counted twelve choir Sisters and seven lay Sisters. The Sisters of St. Joseph of Paris, Rouen, Toulouse, d'Agen, Limoges, and Rochelle are branches of the house at Bordeaux, but all these houses have different costumes and rules introduced by the bishops of the various dioceses. Mademoiselle Delpech herself founded the house at Paris, and gave it the name of Divine Providence. She died there in 1674.

There are in Paris the Sisters called Daughters of St. Joseph of Providence. Bishop Francis Harlay gave them constitutions, edited at Paris in 1694. Those of Bordeaux were edited there in 1708. Those of Rouen, printed at Rouen in 1696, were entitled "Constitutions of the Daughters Hospitallers of the Congregation of St. Joseph for the Instruction of Orphans." The house at Bordeaux during the French Revolution in 1790 shared the fate of its sister institutions. We learn from the oral testimony of two city officials, who had in possession the archives of the Gironde, that this convent then contained fourteen choir Sisters and four lay Sisters, with eighteen pupils boarding in the house. It contained a large chapel fronting on St. Eulalie Street. The same archives had duplicate deeds of convent property in the name of superiors of the orphan girls at Bordeaux: Louis Teste, in 1643; Iabean Mauriet, in 1655; Elizabeth Margaret Mackarty, in 1790. The first deed was for a purchase on June 19, 1630, by Margaret Bethome, widow of Raymond de Massip, M.P., of a house and lot on St. Eulalie Street, for the establishment of a house for the Servants of the Poor Orphan Girls of Bordeaux. This was evidently the commencement of the foundation which was sanctioned and became a regular community in 1638. Many modern writers have erred in designating the work of Mademoiselle Delpech, Madame de Massip, and Cardinal Sourdis as the actual origin of the Congregation of the Sisters of St. Joseph at Bordeaux.

The house at Rochelle, founded by Sisters who went from Bordeaux in 1659, adopted the constitutions of Cardinal Sourdis in 1664. At that time the members of this house wished to form a regular congregation, under the name of Daughters of the Trinity, called religious of the Congregation of St. Joseph. Their rules, which bear a special seal, were printed at Paris in 1664, under the title of "The Institution, Rules, and Constitutions of the Daughters of the Trinity." A third institute, under the name of Hospitallers of St. Joseph, was founded in 1642 by Mademoiselle Marie de la Tere, of a distinguished family of Flèche of Anjou. This pious lady commenced her good work by taking care of the poor in the hospital at Flèche, and was joined the same year by Mademoiselle Ribere, maid-of-honor to the Princess Condé. They were soon assisted by twelve others, and on the 25th of October, 1653, they adopted the constitutions of Claude de Rueil, Bishop of Angers. In 1652 they were applied for at Laval à Bauge and à Moulines, and in 1659 they founded a house in Montreal, Canada. These Sisters of St. Joseph at first made four simple and temporary vows, the fourth of which was to employ themselves in the care of the poor; but in 1663 they commenced to make perpetual vows and to observe enclosure. Alexander VII. approved their institute, under the rules of St. Augustine, by a brief of January 9, 1666, sanctioned by the French parliament August 30, 1667; and Henry Arnand, Bishop of Angers, gave them the constitutions in 1655. They established themselves at Nîmes in 1663, at Avignon in 1670, at Beaufort in 1674, at Isle in 1683, and Rivire and Languedoc in 1700.

The Hospitallers of St. Joseph were re-established at Nîmes in 1803.

Neither the Sisters of St. Joseph founded at Puy in 1650, who sent out missions to Lyons, Bourg, Bordeaux, and Annecy, nor the Sisters of St. Joseph organized at Cluny in 1807, are included in the Sisters Hospitallers mentioned in this note.

II.

Letters-patent of Monseigneur Henry de Maupas, Bishop of Puy, Count of Vellay, for the establishment of the Congregation of the Sisters of St. Joseph.

WE, Henry de Maupas of Tours, Bishop and Lord of Puy, Count of Vellay, immediate suffragan of his holiness, Abbot of St. Denis of Rheims, Councillor of the King in his Council, Almoner of the Queen Regent, desirous of the advancement of the glory of God, and the salvation of souls, and the practice of works of charity in our diocese, have learned that some pious widows and young girls wish to consecrate themselves to laudable exercises of charity, such as the service of the great hospital of the sick poor of our city, and for the direction and education of orphan girls of our asylum at Montferrand; and to apply themselves with more leisure to the above said exercises, they desire, under our good pleasure and our approbation, to establish a society and congregation in which, living in community, they can leisurely, without other hindrance, employ themselves in the above said services This design seems so praiseworthy that we have approved it with great pleasure. We have permitted and will permit the above said widows and young girls to erect their congregation under the name and title of Daughters of St Joseph, to assemble and to live in community in one or in many houses, according as they may find necessary for the better propagation)f the fruits of their charity, and to multiply the above said houses in all the places of our diocese where we judge proper. And that all things be carried out with more order, and that the said new congregation may prosper, we have framed and given rules to the above said young girls and widows, which they shall keep exactly for the greater glory of God and the edification of their neighbor, and also that they undertake the charge of the aforesaid hospital of Montferrand. Taking the above-mentioned widows and young girls ànd their congregation under our protection, we ordain that our vicars and officials take in hand this praiseworthy enterprise, and do all in their power to promote its good and to protect the members of the congregation, to whom we give our blessing and invoke the blessing of God the Father, the Son, and the Holy Ghost.

    HENRY, Bishop of Puy,
           Per GERARDIN.

PUY, March 10, 1651.

www.ingramcontent.com/pod-product-compliance
Lightning Source LLC
Chambersburg PA
CBHW020223240426
43672CB00006B/396